SOCIAL STUDIES MATTERS
TEACHING AND LEARNING WITH AUTHENTICITY

29 28 27 26 25 24 23 22   1 2 3 4 5

Published by Gibbs Smith Education
P.O. Box 667
Layton, UT 84041
801.544.9800
www.gibbssmitheducation.com

Publisher: Jared L. Taylor
Editorial Director: Elizabeth Wallace
Managing Editor: Michelle DeVries
Author: Emily Schell
Editor: Giacomo J. Calabria
Cover design: Dennis Wunsch
Photo Editor: Anna-Morgan Leonards
Copyeditor: Heather Kerrigan

Gibbs Smith books are printed on either recycled, 100% post-consumer
waste, FSC-certified papers, or on paper produced from a 100% certified
sustainable forest/controlled wood source.

Printed and bound in the U.S.A.
ISBN: 978-1-4236-5801-6

CONTENTS

INTRODUCTION

"Yes, in all my research, the greatest leaders looked inward and were able to tell a good story with authenticity and passion."

—Deepak Chopra

As a new teacher many years ago, I realized that I was woefully unprepared to teach social studies to my fourth and fifth grade students. Looking back at my professional preparation program, there was no course required or even available at my university to prepare me for this subject. In fact, I wasn't quite sure what the subject entailed and did not know what was expected of me as a teacher of social studies. I was confident about teaching the other disciplines in my self-contained elementary class, but I needed help with social studies. So I sought out and attended any and all professional development related to the subject. There was not a lot available in my school district and region, but I found some workshops, meetings, institutes, and a professional organization to help.

Soon, I was hooked! I felt as though I had uncovered a secret treasure trove, and I wondered why this subject did not receive the same attention, time, and resources as English language arts, mathematics, science, physical education, and the arts. I discovered the value, importance, enormity, and joy of teaching social studies. I also recognized the responsibility I held as a teacher to ensure that students understand who they are (culturally, socially, politically), where they are (physically, relatively, chronologically), and how they might navigate this ever-changing world with personal success. When I spoke with my colleagues about my newfound passion for teaching social studies, I noticed a kind of glazed-over look in their eyes. "That's nice" was a typical response as I tried to engage others in idea sharing and peer coaching. However, I soon found myself doing what we do not want teachers to do—I closed my door and did my thing.

My students and I traveled around the world and across time through great stories found in our textbook, primary sources, historical fiction, documentaries, historical reenactors, field trips, simulations, games, and guest speakers. We tracked our journeys with maps, pictures, and stories of our own. We processed and presented information through Socratic seminars, journal writing, small group and whole class discussions, projects, murals, multimedia, and pen pals. There never seemed to be enough time for social studies, and so we integrated it into other subjects where it was possible to do so.

After a few years, I moved schools. I realized I was doing something right when my new principal stopped by to observe what was happening in our sixth-grade classroom. She said that students were talking about their studies of ancient Egypt while waiting for the school gates to open in the morning. Apparently, she said, this is not a typical topic of conversation for preteens waiting to start the day. I asked a student to show Mrs. Walker around the classroom (because the tour is always more authentic when led by a student) so she could see what learning about ancient Egypt looked like in our classroom. The student explained how the class traveled on a simulated airplane and used maps to find the location, routes to, and surrounding area of Egypt. He shared his journal entry from that "flight" filled with predictions and anticipation for this new adventure (i.e., unit) in ancient Egypt. He led her into the class pyramid painfully constructed with butcher paper "stones" in the reading corner and he introduced her to the sarcophagus and surrounding mummies with canopic jars. The student explained funerary customs and religious beliefs as cultural elements of ancient Egyptians—depicted in the hieroglyphics and student-made artifacts inside the pyramid—as well as the political and social structures that included pharaohs, scribes, merchants, farmers, and enslaved people. The student pointed out books, artifacts, and documents that he and classmates found useful in piecing together the history and significance of Egyptian people. He added that while there are well-known people from this period acknowledged for their leadership and achievements, the class realized it is just as important to study the lives and contributions of the people whose names were never recorded in historical records.

As I developed my skills as a social studies teacher, I learned from many others who presented at conferences, wrote books, and served as mentors. I was eager to learn more and be the best possible teacher for my students. I knew that I needed to continue learning about history, geography, governments, and economic principles in addition to identifying best practices for teaching and learning history and the social sciences. I knew that I needed to develop instructional plans that were engaging, meaningful, and relevant. I needed to create lessons that invited students into their learning and allowed them to see the value of social studies education as they produced work that accurately reflects their exploration, ideas, and progress. I wanted students to be the center of their social studies lessons and always be asking, "What does this have to do with me?" In doing so, they would be able to recognize and use their cultural wealth to build their own agency and develop pathways to civic engagement. They would identify and build out the connections of their standards-based content to the real-world context in which they lived. They would continue making plans for their futures as scholars, workers, leaders, innovators, and citizens in communities making positive contributions to the common good.

After more than 30 years in education, including high school and preservice methods courses in social studies, I continue to learn and grow as a social studies educator. Mostly, I have learned that time and experience in this work does not mean ascending to a certain height or proficiency level. I have learned that successful educators remain in constant motion—climbing up and down a ladder depending on who their students are, what they are teaching, what is happening in local communities and the world, how new research informs practice, and what resources are available for learning, including technologies, materials, and programs. In other words, teaching social studies is a dynamic endeavor that continues to embrace change. All teachers are familiar with change and manage their lessons, nurture their classroom culture, and respond to students differently over time (even period to period) because factors rarely stay the same. Therefore, this analogy of moving up and down a ladder should resonate well.

You might ask, "Why do we have to move up and down a ladder? Why can't we just teach in the ways we know best?" To extend the analogy a bit further, think about when and why you use a ladder. If you are like me, you need to access something out of reach or you are making home improvements and need some help when attending to the highest points in a room or on a building. Now think about what this means for students who find social studies lessons "out of reach" in your classroom. Or consider improvements to your curriculum, instruction, and assessments when you and your students question missing voices and multiple perspectives in their studies. A ladder would be helpful to provide access and make needed improvements.

If we have learned anything from recent years during which we endured a global pandemic, witnessed the effects of climate change, and a resurgence of social justice movements such as Black Lives Matter, #MeToo, and Stop AAPI Hate; then we know that improvements to what and how we teach social studies are necessary. Student engagement is no longer a goal, but a necessity. Students must learn how to evaluate claims of "fake news" and understand how to make decisions based on reliable evidence and factual information. Entire communities need to understand the differences between teaching standards-based history and social sciences related to institutions and racism, culturally sustaining pedagogy, and critical race theory.

If they are to become our future leaders, innovators, consumers, and influencers, they need to realize that they have the potential to be all of these things today. However, successful leaders, innovators, consumers, and influencers will have the knowledge, disposition, and skills developed in effective social studies programs. Those programs must inform and build background, focus on details while recognizing the greater context, require complex and challenging work each day, center students with all of their cultural and unique experiences, and provide opportunities for the teacher to bring authenticity into the learning environment through the decisions they make, implement, and evaluate as professional educators.

As you read and discuss this book, I invite you to climb up and down this ladder to consider, analyze, utilize, and assess ideas that promote authentic learning in social studies. This might mean changing some of your instructional practices, resources, or projects. Or this could mean adding components to the structure of your social studies program. Let me leave you with one more consideration for what might be called the ladder of authentic learning: At times, we use ladders to move from one place to another. As you think about where you are now in your teaching of social studies and reflect on the ideas presented in the coming chapters, will you climb the ladder to find a different place for social studies—a place that honors and respects the content, context, work, student, and teacher through authentic learning?

Enjoy your continuous journey as a social studies educator. I look forward to meeting you along the path or at one of those pit stops that offer relief, refreshment, and fellowship.

This introduction ends with a feature you will find at the beginning of each chapter—a thought-provoking quote. It just seems to fit best here, and comes from one of my teachers who regularly guides me in meditation and reflection. Teaching, as you know, has the ability to drain us of our patience, creativity, and physical and emotional energy. Deepak Chopra helps me to keep my reservoir full by reminding me to look within, breathe deeply, and tap into my authenticity as an educator, mother, sister, friend, environmentalist, global citizen, and human being. I am continually learning how to make my work as an educator energize me in ways that add to—rather than deplete— my all-important reservoir. And so, I trust you will find this book full of "good stories" that are all shared with authenticity and passion with the intention of inspiring and guiding you to generate your own stories about teaching social studies with authenticity.

Authentic Learning Ladder

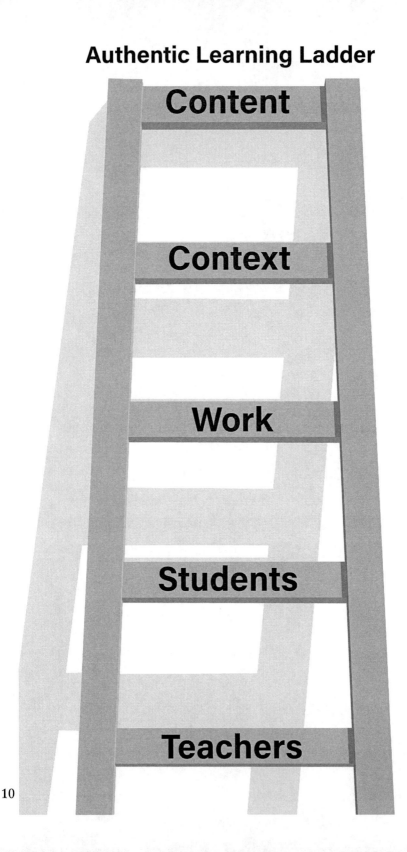

SECTION 1

SETTING THE STAGE FOR SOCIAL STUDIES

SECTION 1: SETTING THE STAGE FOR SOCIAL STUDIES

Chapter 1
What is Authenticity in Social Studies?

"Aspire to be authentic." —Yann Martel

Student engagement remains an issue for teachers of social studies. What can be done to stimulate students' attention and fuel their interest, curiosity, and exploration of history, geography, economics, and civics/government? How can teachers present social studies in ways that engage students during lessons, throughout a course, and beyond the classroom?

This book is meant to help teachers answer these questions—and more—as they consider *authenticity* in the content and practices of social studies. The term *"authentic"* has many meanings, including accurate, genuine, reliable, true, truthful, trustworthy, and dependable. Consider the level of engagement when students are actively interrogating the accuracy and reliability of the material presented in their social studies classes. Imagine students developing the knowledge and skills to determine the dependability of sources embedded into their textbooks and the reliability of authors, cartographers, and historians as well as politicians, scientists, and community leaders. Allowing students to bring their own lived experiences, unique perspectives, and cultural wealth into each lesson positions them as essential to the success of the lesson. If this became standard practice in the social studies classroom, now consider the trust and motivation in students who earnestly want to learn more about the world in which they live through stories of the past, representations of places and culture, and evidence of civic engagement locally and globally.

Finally, think about what this could mean for teachers who bring authenticity to their teaching and reveal the range of thoughts and feelings that accompany their own learning as they process information related to the choices, decisions, and consequences faced by people over time and place. Social studies classrooms could become safe and brave spaces for teachers and students to investigate and learn from the many challenges, achievements, and complexities of what it means to be human. Furthermore, students would detect in their teachers the care, concern, and commitment to such values as civic engagement and responsibility, human rights, justice and equality, and the common good.

We are teaching and learning during a time of unrest and uncertainty. Today's news stories have deep roots in local and national history, policies and institutions developed by governments and organizations, and sustained cultural beliefs and practices. Whether students are following the news or not, this is the reality of their world today. Authentic social studies acknowledges current events as an entry point for exploring the historic, economic, geographic, or legal context to an issue while also providing students with opportunities to identify and understand root causes, cause and effect, chronology, spatial reasoning, cost-benefit analyses, and other important skills embedded in social studies. In other words, authentic social studies relies on the bridges that must be built between today's real-world events and the events of the past. This also holds true for bridging studies of people, places, and events in the local environment to those in distant and global environments. It is easy to say "Keep it real" while teaching social studies because we know that the content is based in reality. However, a better guiding thought might be, "Keep it real for the students."

Keeping it real for students can translate to using a 21st-century lens on studies of the past and attending to current events in local, national, and global communities. It can also mean teaching from a stance of practical value for students. Teachers might ask themselves, "What do students want and need from my course?" Better yet, teachers might ask their students, "What do *you* want and need from this social studies course?" In evaluating their responses, teachers may be motivated to learn even more about their students from the students themselves. This beginning-of-the-year exercise can reveal enough information for teachers to better orient their lessons and overall plans for keeping social studies real for their students. For example, teachers may find that many students cannot relate to the content presented and therefore embrace culturally responsive pedagogy and practices. Students might reveal that a continuous cycle of reading-lecture-worksheet-writing-test is "boring" and inspire teachers to instead use inquiry methodologies. Students might also express a concern about the relevance and usefulness of social studies, which may spark ideas in the teacher to add a "rationale" to each lesson plan and challenge students to end each lesson with their ideas about the usefulness of the knowledge, skills, and questions developed during the lesson. Keeping track of these ideas (in a journal, class chart, digital portfolio, collage, etc.) over time can produce thoughtful discussions, writing, arguments, murals, and testimonies related to the relevance of social studies education. Furthermore, students' dispositions about learning, critical thinking, inquiry, evidence, documentation, storytelling, perspectives, and communication may shift as *they* recognize the value of the subject.

Keeping it real for students also means paying attention to the tools, challenges, and issues of the 21st century. Today's students are considered digital natives—born into and growing up in a world of digital technologies that make computers, applications, and Internet access a way of life. While disparities in equity and access to digital technologies in the United States and around the world persists, digital tools and communications are fundamental to the personal, school, and work lives of our students. They do not relate to paper, bound books, folded maps, and No. 2 pencils like many of us who are not digital natives. And we might not relate to video games, social media, YouTube, hacking, spoofing, cryptocurrency, and cyberbullying like many of our students who are digital natives. Transporting students to a different time and place to understand the extreme conditions faced by early explorers or the risks involved when people stood against their governments, employers, and neighbors to fight for their rights remains a challenge for teachers who might actually find the tools and issues of today's digital natives to be assets in meeting that challenge. For example, identifying the physical, emotional, and economic conditions faced by early explorers who traveled by land or by water can be compared to the experiences of students who are early adopters of modern technologies, such as distance learning, 3D printing, 5G networks, TikTok, and artificial intelligence. Projecting into their futures, what conditions will our students face with advancements in all-electric or driverless cars, extended reality, human augmentation, civilian spaceflight, drone home deliveries, and artificial general intelligence? These are the new frontiers of exploration in the 21st century.

Today's issues extend beyond and also relate to modern technologies. Some have remained present for generations, including human rights, food security, poverty, gender equality, and disease and health care. Others have emerged as a result of past actions taken, such as climate change, terrorism, and refugees. Capitalizing on accessible information through social media, multiple news sources, remote imaging, and personal communications via computers, tablets, and mobile phones allows for greater sharing of information, wider perspectives and experiences presented, and immediate attention to issues for individuals, communities, organizations, and officials. Social studies teachers have multiple opportunities to fold these issues into their standards-based curriculum to help students unpack current issues while learning about the history and systems that created or contributed to them. Making these connections can be the work of both teachers and students who collaborate to inquire, gather and corroborate evidence, analyze data, and draw conclusions to build an argument.

Establishing a culture of inquiry, investigation, and exploration in a social studies class centers students as both learners and subjects. This is their history, and they are learning about their laws, communities, cultures, economies, political structures, social systems, and environments as well as those of others. By embedding students in their own lessons, their studies are no longer about people they don't know and cannot relate to. Cultural relevance can be achieved in addition to support for civic engagement. Students can enter their social studies education with questions about fake news, political discord, bipartisan politics, social justice, and systemic racism. Teachers can integrate media literacy, social emotional learning, trauma-informed practices, culturally responsive teaching, environmental literacy, and global competence into their existing curriculum.

Fortunately, there is no single recipe for effective and authentic teaching of social studies. That means teachers have a lot of options to choose from when creating learning experiences that are engaging and relevant for their students—choices related to content resources, instructional practices, projects and activities, etc. Anyone who tells you there is "one best way" for students to learn social studies needs to revisit the meaning of authenticity and consider the multiple perspectives—of the content as well as the learners—embedded in every lesson. Invite your students to keep the learning authentic in your class by leading a discussion about what it means to be authentic and identify the many ways that learning can remain authentic through the content, context, and work products. Most importantly, students and teachers can keep each other in check when it comes to being authentic throughout the learning process. Bringing your genuine interests, questions, concerns, and lived experiences into the social studies classroom will make for robust and productive learning experiences.

SECTION 2
AUTHENTIC PLANNING

SECTION 2: AUTHENTIC PLANNING

Chapter 2
Exploring Real Issues: Time, Standards, and Authentic Learning

"Authenticity is more than speaking; Authenticity is also about doing. Every decision we make says something about who we are."

—Simon Sinek

Where to begin? Social studies teachers typically start their school year knowing which grade level(s) and what general course content they will be teaching. Where do they go from there in the planning process?

For many, this effort begins with a look at the course outline (if available), adopted standards and framework, course text and materials, and any required assessments used by the school or district. It is helpful to know what students are expected to learn in your course and what resources are provided for their learning. Another important factor to consider is *time*. How much time is devoted to your social studies program or course? Is there a time requirement established for your course or grade-level expectation for the amount of time spent teaching and learning social studies? Some elementary teachers assign social studies to one-half of the year while teaching science during the other half. Some secondary schools offer one-semester social studies courses in their block schedules. Some teachers integrate social studies with English language arts into a humanities course. All these factors—independently as well as collectively—are important for teachers to consider in planning for authentic teaching and learning.

Let's consider, for example, an existing course outline. Who developed the outline and for what purpose? When was the outline created and under what circumstances? We have seen many changes in our schools and in social studies education during the past 10–20 years, and schools across the country have responded differently to those changes. From the introduction of national standards in the early 1990s to the College, Career, and Civic Life (C3) Framework for social studies State Standards in 2013, attention to what and how we teach the subject has shifted with varying responses from states adopting their own standards, frameworks, and assessments. Some schools, districts, and states have changed their policies and practices around social studies assessments. Some continue to use benchmark or end-of-course examinations and others maintain a standards-based test requirement. Some schools have abandoned testing altogether in favor of an exhibition-type event for students to present their projects and receive feedback from peers, teachers, administrators, and members of the local community.

The greater context of education has influenced changes as well, drawing our attention and practices to address universal design for learning, English language development and multilingual learning, differentiated instruction, depth of knowledge, inquiry-based instruction, social and emotional learning, technologies in the classroom, cultural relevance, and more. We have spent years addressing disciplinary literacy, problem- and project-based learning, document-based questions, and now inquiry arcs. We could spend the rest of this book examining each of these influences on social studies education and exploring how they created lasting impacts on how and what we teach today. However, I trust you will bring these (and other) issues into your consideration of any existing course outline or course of study document that guides your social studies planning and instruction. Some of the outlines in use today across schools and districts are outdated and contribute to inauthentic teaching and learning. The world, our profession, our students, and the content of social studies continues to evolve. It is incumbent on all of us to work together, stay abreast of these changes, share ideas and resources, and provide the collegial support necessary for social studies to remain meaningful and relevant.

If your aim is authentic teaching and learning in social studies, the documents and principles that guide your course structure, curriculum, and pedagogy must reflect the changes that have moved this discipline into the 21st century. Consider these shifts:

From	To
Teacher-centered	Student-centered
Independent learning and assessment	Cooperative and collaborative learning, assessments, and reflection
Focus on discrete knowledge and skills	Integrated, thematic, connected learning
Primarily lecture, reading, and writing	A variety of engaging strategies that utilize and develop multiple skills beyond reading, writing, and listening (e.g., speaking, reasoning, spatial, social and emotional, evaluation, computational, media literacy, etc.)

From	To
Bound information resources and limited tools	Multiple and differentiated learning resources that go beyond the textbook and library reference materials (e.g., oral histories, images, film, artifacts, maps, data, etc.) and available tools (e.g., audio, image, and video recorders; apps for data collection and analysis; on-demand satellite images; GIS for interactive maps and digital mapmaking; online archives, etc.)
Predominantly Euro-centric perspectives presented in primary and secondary text, images, maps, and documentation	Inclusion of multiple perspectives and intentional attention to "missing voices" while studying power dynamics throughout history

Beyond the changes in social studies education are the many ways in which our world has changed. Does your course outline reflect research and changes in human activity related to the climate crisis and environmental sustainability; social justice and human rights; technology and engineering; diseases, treatments, and health; migration, refugees, and resettlement; population and resources; and conflict, terrorism, security, and peacekeeping?

For example, the ways in which we acquire and communicate information today is far different from the ways people of the past obtained and shared information. Students need to think deeply about how communication has changed over time in form, function, and accessibility. Using a 21st-century lens on how people record, store, and share information today will not help them understand that literacy in many cultures—now and in the past—has been limited and often reserved for people of a certain class and gender. Those in power have controlled the information both shared during their time and left behind for historical record. They monitored what, where, and how information was recorded and who received information. From ancient royalty and their official scribes long ago to average citizens and their social media accounts today, the world of information and communications has changed dramatically. Why does this matter? Consider the implications of who maintains the power and authority to generate, access, and disburse information. With that information, people make decisions about where and how they live their lives. Without that information, people are subject to mistreatment, exploitation, and oppression. Information is a precious commodity and an important resource. Communications are the systems that allow for either democratic or restricted exchange of those resources.

Therefore, we should not be surprised when students today question the information packaged and presented to them in a traditional educational setting. Teachers need to consider how students acquire and share information differently now than in the past. Textbooks are no longer the sole or main source of historical, geographic, and economic information. Students are carrying a wealth of information around in their pockets accessible with a smartphone and decent Wi-Fi connection. To achieve authentic teaching and learning, a course outline should reflect not only the content knowledge presented in standards and frameworks, but skills that help students access, analyze, evaluate, corroborate, and use that information in ways that develop critical thinking, inquiry, and collaboration. Students will be able to search online for names, dates, and locations of historic events. Students in authentic learning environments will be able to evaluate those sources found online and in their textbooks, identify additional sources that allow for deeper understanding and multiple viewpoints, and use that information to build and defend arguments that introduce new perspectives on the events and generate inquiries that extend beyond that moment in time. The course, using this example, would integrate media literacy skills throughout so students can effectively interrogate and corroborate that information. A course outline that identifies topics, page numbers in the textbook, and assignments designed to summarize the content presented is certainly outdated and insufficient for today's students.

While some textbooks and materials introduce connections between social studies content and the modern world, this should be a consistent feature for learning in a course outline and classroom practices. Some teachers integrate current events into their courses through *CNN Student News* and various broadcast news services, *Newsela* and other print news sources, and NPR's *Up First* and similar podcasts. These accessible resources allow students to learn about and discuss the real-world people, places, and events that draw our attention today while studying about people, places, and events of importance in the past. Students are able to witness history in the making through current events while better understanding and investigating policies, laws, conflict, cultural influences, social issues, environmental impact, and economic principles. Consistently providing real-world connections for students through current events activities, examples used in lessons, and inviting students to share their own related experiences and examples will engage you and your students in authentic learning. Consider who to invite into your classroom (in person or virtually) as a guest presenter or discussion facilitator. Additionally, think about the projects assigned to students as opportunities for them to engage with real-world information, events, people, and places that will enhance their knowledge and skills development.

In the process of helping students connect the past with the present and distant places with the local environment, teachers are guiding students to explore and learn about the world in which they currently live. Students have long questioned the purpose of studying year after year about people who are no longer living and in conditions that no longer exist. While it is interesting to learn about cultural traditions across time and place or weapons and strategies used in wars, many students struggle to find the value in social studies. As you follow the standards and frameworks that guide the general content of your social studies course, consider ways for students to learn about the things that relate to life today and challenges of tomorrow. Think about the cultural universals or big ideas that transcend time and place. For example, food can be considered a cultural universal while "people need food to survive" is a big idea. Whether students are learning about early humans, ancient civilizations, medieval societies, or people and events of the modern era, they can relate to the elements that are basic needs, such as food. While providing some relatable or unrelatable examples of how food was accessed, prepared, and consumed—and what foods they ate—students could be learning about issues of food security and insecurity. Or, they could study the relationship between food consumption and a healthy diet. Both of these examples have important connections to real-world issues that surface across local communities in the United States and around the world today. Without taking students off-track from the standards-based course of study, building these connections to the present time and local environment helps students to see the value in social studies. They can become more critically aware of what it means to be human over time and place, realizing that people have common needs and challenges and use different approaches and resources to satisfy those needs and overcome those challenges. Students can also begin to apply these lessons to their own lives as they think more deeply and strategically about the importance of healthy, sustainable, and reliable access to food for themselves, their families, and their communities. When students start to recognize food waste and food insecurity in their school, home, or community after studying about peasants, enslaved people, or the Great Depression, they are making important connections. Beyond making connections while studying, students can prepare for taking action through their own choices and behaviors.

The world continues to change in many ways. Through your course of study, you can allow students to understand that change is a constant in life, and that people respond to change in different ways. Conditions caused by the global COVID-19 pandemic can best illustrate this fact and students can unpack in real time the fears and anxiety, frustrations and resolve, and resiliency of human beings when confronted with a crisis that has far-reaching and deadly outcomes. People around the world have responded differently to lockdown and mask mandates, travel restrictions, quarantines, and vaccinations. Laws and policies have changed frequently as scientific evidence and updated data emerges. News cycles remain fixated on statistics, stories, and announcements. Businesses closed and others transformed the ways they conduct business. Courts and public institutions closed too. Parks, theaters, and concert venues were no longer accessible and then reopened with limitations. Schools converted from in-person to virtual to hybrid and back to in-person instruction (with new and changing rules and requirements). As educators tried to help students focus on their course content, programs and considerations were introduced to address trauma, social and emotional learning, and stress and anxiety.

I cannot think of a better example to help our students recognize the role of change in our world. With change comes the issues of uncertainty and ambiguity, with which we have all lived during the pandemic years. As teachers of history, we cannot ignore these issues as prominent in each and every crisis experienced by small and large groups of human beings since the beginning of time. And so, we need to teach with these important realities in mind. From our minds to our course syllabi, units, and daily lessons, we can be intentional and focused in ensuring that our students understand universal truths, or the "big ideas" of the human condition, while studying specific people, events, eras, places, and concepts in our social studies classes.

How does this look? It's not as neat and compartmentalized as we have seen in traditional course outlines or scope and sequence documents. Bringing authenticity into your course planning, instruction, and assessments can seem a bit messy as it is blended into student learning in different ways that depend on you, your students, and how you manage your time. Developing and using a lens on authentic learning is what will allow you to make necessary adjustments to your course outline, instructional planning and delivery, and assessments. This lens will become evident to students as your interventions, questions, discussions, and assignments reflect what is meaningful, relatable, and relevant for all.

SECTION 2: AUTHENTIC PLANNING

Chapter 3
High Expectations for Rigor and Relevance

"When you are real in your music, people know it and they feel your authenticity."

—Wynonna Judd

Let us begin with a thought exercise: Imagine yourself as a student in a social studies classroom . . . sitting in the same seat . . . in the same room . . . learning the same things that your parents did decades before you. And they sat in the same seats . . . in the same classrooms . . . learning the same things that their parents did decades before them. Maybe there are different teachers and hopefully there are updated textbooks. However, the content and probably the methods of learning in these social studies classes remain the same generation after generation.

How did you feel during that exercise? If you are like me, it did not feel very encouraging. It made me feel as though I was going through the motions, "playing the game," paying my dues as a student. I imagined that there was a predetermined outcome for me that was the same for every student who sat in this class before me. I did not feel as though I had anything to bring into the learning process, and that my job was to soak up whatever the teacher and textbook wanted me to absorb. I was made to feel that this is just the way school works.

Alternatively, maybe you thought, "Wow! Teachers have really perfected the teaching of social studies and there is no need for any change." However, if that were the case, I do not think you would have picked up this book. And let me remind you that student engagement remains an issue for social studies teachers everywhere (see Chapter 1).

Truthfully, the above statements just about sum up my education experiences from elementary to high school. I saw school as something that I was supposed to do, but I was not sure why. I could understand the value of learning to read and write, but I had no clue as to why science or history or mathematics was important or useful. Fortunately, I did well in school because I paid attention in class, figured out how to study, and learned how to please my teachers. Yes, I was *that* student who volunteered to sharpen pencils, clean the boards, and put up the chairs. But I did not know why we had to learn about George Washington and the Civil War or memorize the preamble to the Constitution and Gettysburg Address. I did not know what to do with any of the information presented in my social studies classes. I read, listened, took tests, and moved on to the next topic. Nothing seemed connected or relevant to me.

There were two exceptions that I remember distinctly because they disrupted the normal cadence of lecture, reading, and note-taking in class. In 1976, my eighth-grade US history teacher announced that there was a presidential election between Jimmy Carter and Gerald Ford. Mr. LeMay explained that we were going to hold a mock election in class, which meant learning about the candidates and their platforms as well as the duties of the US president and our election process. We paid attention to the news, held interesting discussions about real issues, and voted in our first presidential (mock) election! Later, in 10th grade world history, my teacher explained that we were going to do something different in class. Mr. Sutton instructed us to work in small groups to figure out a dilemma that involved several people stranded on a sinking boat. In order to keep the boat from sinking, we had to determine which person should be thrown overboard. Each person had a profile and I remember arguing with my classmates about the importance of priests and mothers. I did not care for that scenario, but enjoyed listening to and debating with my peers. Later, we repeated the exercise by deciding who would be best to travel into space and colonize a new planet. Those activities stand out in my social studies learning experiences because they took us out of our routine of lecture, notes, reading, and writing essays. And those activities were hard! They were more challenging than hunting for answers in the textbook and writing them down on a worksheet. In hindsight, we were being introduced to sociology, philosophy, psychology, and ethics while developing our skills of reasoning, argumentation, persuasion, and logic.

How do you want your students to feel as they sit in their seats in your social studies classroom? Imagine your students sitting in the same seats as their parents did decades ago. Are your students learning the same general lessons that their parents learned? If so, and your students recognize this fact, consider how they might feel knowing this.

How can we help students see their uniqueness and important contributions to a community of learners? How can we provide a safe space for students to learn about and practice civic engagement so they can develop the necessary knowledge, skills, and disposition to be actively engaged in their communities outside of the classroom?

Your answers to these questions are situated squarely in authentic teaching and learning. Social studies is the place for students—as early as kindergarten—to better understand who they are as individuals, members of communities, and citizens of their state, nation, and world. They learn these ongoing lessons in the contexts of history, physical and cultural geography, economics, sociology, anthropology, psychology, civics, and government or political science. Your answers should also resonate with this overarching question that should be asked—frequently—by all teachers: "What are my expectations for my students?"

I hear a lot of teachers explain their high expectations for students and the rigor of their course. Many interpret this as a large quantity of material that students should consume and reflect back accurately in tests, essays, discussions, and projects. Whether teaching Advanced Placement, International Baccalaureate, advanced, honors, or Gifted and Talented Education courses or not, social studies teachers understand the depth and breadth of their discipline, which requires a great deal of time and effort for teaching and learning. Often, teachers will refer to the stamina that needs to be built in order for students to keep up with the material and fast pace of the class, which covers a lot of ground due to the standards and course outline. Most secondary teachers who teach only social studies courses have a deep and abiding passion for their subject matter, and want to inspire their students to appreciate and embrace social studies the way they have done. This can be done skillfully throughout the grade levels as students begin to realize that social studies is about them, their families, neighbors (locally and globally), and friends as well as the places, systems, and events that fill our world with meaning, value, and opportunity. And the doorway into these studies is curiosity.

If students view social studies as a tome of old information that they have to tackle each year in order to pass tests and make passing grades to fulfill a school requirement, they will find little joy or enthusiasm for their studies. Achieving those high expectations established by their teachers will be challenging and frustrating. Establishing a foundation of curiosity with students who are introduced to authentic learning about people, places, institutions, and events can pique student interest and guide them into their studies with questions, ideas, and opinions that become an important part of the class.

As we continue to explore high expectations for learning and rigor in the social studies classroom, I feel the need to pause and address one of the challenging issues that emerged in my own research with teachers. That is the issue of fun. First, let me state for the record that I am a big fan of fun, and I believe that my former students will testify that I can definitely bring fun into the classroom. However, when fun becomes the goal of social studies, I have a problem. "I just want my students to see social studies as fun" has been stated to me while teachers describe their use of engaging strategies, such as simulations, games, and hands-on activities. There are many wonderful methods to draw students into their learning, help them through their learning, and assess what they have learned. Jeopardy games, character interpretation, assembly lines, churning butter, *The Oregon Trail*, and panning for gold are all examples of fun and engaging activities. However, these should not be the sole goal of a social studies program. Students across the grade levels who had these experiences in their social studies classes have told me about participating in these activities, and while I listened carefully, there was very little description about the content or skills gained. I know we can effectively combine fun and engaging instruction with rigorous and effective learning.

Social studies is centered on historical studies. While history cannot be changed in the present, our teaching and student learning of that history can change and has changed. What I am proposing is not to rewrite history as many have argued. *Rewriting history* is defined as being selective about the parts of history or interpreting events in such a way that suits a person's purposes. What I do propose is that we broaden our views of history to be more inclusive and authentic. For example, do we always have to learn from the perspective of those who are privileged and successful? Perhaps we could learn about the roles, struggles, and achievements of those who did not lead the battles, buy the railroads, and sign the founding documents. In addition to learning about those historical figures who stand out in history, we could learn a great deal from those who fought on both sides in the battles as well as those who painstakingly built the railroads and those who were impacted by the founding documents. Students can learn about leadership, technology, and innovation by studying those traditionally highlighted in history lessons. And they can also learn about belief systems, work ethic, and the common good through the studies on average people also included in history.

This type of attention to social studies lessons requires intention and commitment to authentic teaching and learning. It means not just accepting what has always been presented as the people and events of importance, but inquiring about others who were also present and participated in those historical times and places. It means looking beyond the documentation created and preserved for us to study years later, and considering alternative forms of evidence or documentation that is presented in the forms of song, story, art, architecture, and other artifacts.

It is fairly easy for both teachers and students to follow a textbook and review material in the text each day. Raising expectations for teaching and learning requires rigorous planning, instruction, and attention. It means loosening one's control over the narrative and opening space for students to be curious about aspects of social studies that you might not have been prepared to teach. Doing so allows students to bring themselves, with their interests and perspectives, into the areas of study that do relate to them as human beings, citizens, consumers, and contributors to the common good. And this shifts some of the control—of the content and the skills development—from teacher to student, thus raising accountability for students to be fully engaged in their learning through questioning, investigation, gathering and analysis of evidence, evaluation, and communication. In some cases, this type of learning can lead to changes in the students' behaviors, perspectives, and actions.

Let's explore some practical approaches to keeping expectations for students at a high level while maintaining rigor to present appropriate challenges that generate student knowledge and sharpen their skills. You may be familiar with these research-based aspects of effective teaching, and ideally you are integrating these into your instructional practices. As you review these, consider the implications for bringing more authenticity into your teaching. If we are to become more authentic in our teaching and support the authenticity with which students show up each day for learning, we must consider the integration of these approaches to social studies education. And, most importantly, we must commit to knowing who our students are in order for us to address cultural relevance, differentiate instruction, and support student learning styles.

Cultural Relevance

In recent years, we have learned more about culturally responsive, relevant, and sustaining pedagogy. While there are distinctions between these as defined by scholars, including Gloria Ladsen-Billings, Geneva Gay, Django Paris, and H. Samy Alim, they all merit our attention in recognizing that not all students feel represented and valued in our social studies classes.

Culturally responsive pedagogy leverages the strengths that students of color bring into the classroom to make learning more relevant and effective. This requires teachers to recognize the cultural capital and tools that all students bring to school and make use of their cultural learning tools throughout the instructional day.

Culturally relevant pedagogy focuses on student learning and academic success as students develop cultural competence in order to assist in their development of positive ethnic and social identities. Culturally relevant pedagogy supports students' critical consciousness and their abilities to recognize and critique inequities in society.

Culturally sustaining pedagogy affirms and respects key components of assets-based pedagogy while moving beyond acceptance and making connections to cultural knowledge and experiences. Culturally sustaining pedagogy views schools as places where the cultural ways of students of color are sustained rather than ignored or eradicated.

All three approaches emphasize the need to acknowledge and respond appropriately to the assets that accompany each student who enters our classroom every day with their own culture, language, and lived experiences. More importantly, how do we make and sustain a place for all students' cultures to be consistently valued, included, and useful in the learning process? Students bring their authentic selves into our classrooms each day and often leave with feelings of inadequacy, disappointment, and despair because their heritage, language, history, and culture are either absent or dismissed as irrelevant. At times, even their questions are sidelined in efforts to "stay on topic" and on schedule.

Each person's history, culture, and questions are relevant and important. Therefore, each person's history, culture, and questions deserve a place in our social studies classrooms. That does not mean veering from the chronological presentation of state, national, or world history as dictated by state standards. However, it does mean looking differently at how that content is shared with students. Offering connections and comparisons can be helpful while at the same time probing for insights from across time and space.

For example, I spent a lot of time with teachers of early American history who studied in Colonial Williamsburg and wanted to bring colonial history to life with their students in California. Teachers reported concerns about making this content relevant for their many students of Latino/a/x heritage. As I engaged these teachers in discussions about Spanish colonization on the West Coast, which students learned in fourth grade under the topic of "building missions," they started to realize several access points for comparison, context, and connections. In addition, a desire to help students who had immigrated from Latin American countries to learn the history of their new country meant helping those students learn from their existing knowledge base and examples that were more familiar to them. Furthermore, using cooperative learning strategies like "mix, mingle, match" engages students from the position of what they already know to explore learning about people from the past. Here is how we used the strategy:

Each student received an artifact. The artifact was an everyday item, such as a toothbrush, bandage, pen, sticker, matchbook, etc. Half of the students received this item in its modern form. The other half received the item as a replica from the 18th century. For example, the toothbrush was a stick of sassafras root, the bandage a strip of linen, the pen a feather quill, the sticker a wax and stamp, and the matchbook a flint with striker. (All of these items are available for purchase at historic sites.)

Students were asked to analyze their artifact and determine what it was made from, what its use is, and who would use the item.

Students moved around the room to mix and mingle—sharing their items, conclusions, questions, and observations.

Students were instructed to find their 18th century to 21st century match. In other words, there are two toothbrushes in the room, two pens, etc.

Working in pairs, students compared and discussed their items. They were asked to determine the costs and benefits of each version and explain the value of the item (i.e., why people have used that item for hundreds of years).

Each pair was matched up with another pair to share their findings from the previous step. Together, they then compared living in the 18th century to life today. They were instructed to dig a bit deeper to determine who might have had access to their items in the past and in the present. For example, who had a need for a pen in the 18th century and who did not.

This strategy can be adapted for use in other topics of study, and can be used to introduce an instructional unit, enhance themes (e.g., environmental impact, social class, economics, geography, innovation) during the unit, or culminate the unit with review, reflection, discussion, and assessments. All the while, this activity provides students with ways to connect what they know and use today to their studies of people living in different times and places. You might also invite students to bring into class items that serve a particular purpose in order to compare with artifacts or images of items that you have collected. This can work with journal entries, photos, and certificates as well. Find and facilitate strategies that allow students to identify, share, discuss, and learn from their own authentic storehouse of knowledge, experience, insight, and curiosity.

A simpler strategy that can and should be used regularly is "turn and talk." Build into your lessons those intentional moments with clear prompts and instructions for students to turn to a partner, triad, or table group to talk about what they are learning, share authentic examples, and surface questions they might have.

Cultural relevance deserves our attention for many reasons. The structure and content of many social studies courses does not reflect or respect the cultural capital and tools that students bring into our classrooms every day, and we are left wondering why those students are not engaged in ways that we expect. The strategies that fill our lessons must encourage the academic achievement of all students while supporting cultural competence and the development of positive ethnic and social identities. Finally, we must get beyond the celebration months, added examples of people of color, and "oh, yeah" connections. All students deserve an inclusive, representative, genuine social studies program that sustains cultural content, ways of knowing, skills development, language, forms of expression, etc.

Differentiation

We know that each student is unique and enters our classroom with different combinations of knowledge, skills, motivation, and experiences. Carol Tomlinson introduced the concept of differentiation many years ago and maintains that this is a common sense instructional approach to ensuring that every student has the opportunity to succeed to the best of their ability given all of those unique differences. If you are teaching your class using a one-size-fits-all approach, you are definitely not differentiating your instruction. Consider these ways to differentiate social studies.

Content

Your goal is to provide access to the content of your lessons despite differences in background knowledge, literacy skills, and learning styles. Rather than all of your students listening to the same lecture or reading from the same text, identify a variety of resources focused on the content that allows some students to learn through video or film, graphic novels, abbreviated text, audiobooks, podcasts, primary sources, etc. in place of or in addition to the class lecture and text. Some students will find success with course content in ways that other students will not. Maintain your learning targets while differentiating the ways that students reach those targets. This works well for secondary courses that rely on student learning in previous grade levels. Differentiating your content can help students learn or review foundational content that supports their understanding of your course content.

Students can come together to discuss their learning from different sources to become content resources for each other as well. Think about how many times you have talked with others about a historic event even though you all learned information about that event from different resources.

Process

Chances are you arrive at school after taking a different route, moving at a different rate, traveling a different distance, and using a different vehicle than your colleagues. Still, you all ended up in the same place around the same time to do your jobs as teachers. This is one way to describe differentiation of process.

In your classroom, you make assignments for students to complete readings, projects, writing, and other activities. Do all of your students have to complete these assignments using the same guidelines? Think about the students who will be more successful in reaching their learning targets if they could narrate rather than write. Some may require additional time or resources while others less. There are those students who work better with a partner while others prefer to work alone. Some require assistance from notes, resources, and tools, while others can complete assessments and assignments without additional support. Keep in mind that some students have more advantages than others for a variety of reasons. You may have students with jobs outside of school, some care for family members, some have a place to work at home and others do not, some are food insecure, some have moved from school to school while others have stable roots in the school community, some have resources and support at home while others do not, and some have Wi-Fi and computers at home while others must go to a library or borrow from a friend. The differences are vast in how our students are able to address school work. The more options you can provide while maintaining the elements that are critical to the learning goals of your course, the more opportunities you give your students to succeed. You can meet them where they are in respectful and genuine ways.

Products

I remember walking into a classroom that proudly displayed 35 versions of the same project—an arch bridge made from toothpicks glued together. The teacher was so proud, but I had a lot of questions. I learned that students were learning about bridges and their importance during world events. The final product followed instructions provided by the teacher for building a model of an arch bridge.

As you engage your students in projects that result in products, such as a model, think about the students who might interpret the assignment differently and let them create a product that demonstrates learning, but in unanticipated ways. Differentiation of products can present options for students to display their learning using various methods (e.g., write a report, create a multimedia presentation, illustrate a poster). The options can help students to focus on the content rather than the format and select what is comfortable for them. Some students will be better able to showcase their learning by creating an infographic than by writing an essay.

Or, you can make some suggestions about products and allow students to determine the best possible way to respond to the prompt or instructions for demonstrating their learning. In both cases, it is important that you create a scoring guide or rubric that is focused on the content and skills, and not on the format of the product.

Environment

The classroom environment is another way to establish authentic learning while supporting the different needs and learning styles of your students. A classroom with desks in rows projects a message to students that may not be conducive with your efforts to increase student engagement and collaboration. If possible, make adjustments to the way your classroom is designed. Rearrange desks (or have students rearrange the desks during class at appropriate times during the lesson) and create places in the classroom for students to go for resources, a break, a brief discussion, or a place to stretch or sit more comfortably without a desk in their laps. Some classrooms will have a reading corner, a writing station, a listening post, or an art wall. The environment should reflect your acknowledgment that everyone sitting in the same position at the same time is not the goal of education. Your environment should reflect the flexible and differentiated nature of learning and exploration.

This is also an opportunity for you to think about how you present yourself—authentically—to your students. Your classroom can be a reflection of who you are and while you may or may not want to bring in family photos or mementos from home to sit on your desk or bookshelf, you do have an entire room to provide a window into your personality and genuine self. This is a chance to invite your students into your teaching space while sharing this as their learning space. Maybe you cover your bulletin boards with your favorite colors, display your diplomas and certificates, hang some posters of historical figures who inspire you, or cover a wall with maps and photos from your favorite places. Perhaps you invite students to bring in cultural or personal material to display in your classroom. Either way, think about how the space in and around your classroom can be used to differentiate learning in your classroom.

Your class rules and routines are also ways to provide differentiation and demonstrate to your students that you recognize them as individuals who deserve to be treated fairly in their educational setting. Every year, I explained to my students that I would treat them all fairly, but I might not treat them all equally. As we discussed this statement, students realized that equity and fairness are not the same as making everything equal. Because some students had health issues and required additional time and support with their work, the hard and fast deadlines for assignments were not applied to those students. When some students missed class because of family crises, we reorganized our buddy system and project groups. Students need to see flexibility and adaptability and understand why those are applied in order for them to utilize these important skills in their own lives.

Learning Modalities

How do you learn best? Do you have a preferred learning modality (e.g., auditory, visual, kinesthetic, or reading/writing)? Whether or not you ascribe to learning modalities or learning styles, you recognize that people have strong or preferred ways of learning. Learning styles are commonly identified as auditory and musical, visual or spatial, verbal, social or interpersonal, solitary or intrapersonal, physical or kinesthetic, logical, and mathematical.

While we want students to practice and learn all of these ways of learning during their school experiences, students and adults will tell you what their strengths and preferences are. Some want to work independently while others thrive in group work. Some will draw you diagrams, maps, and charts to explain a concept while others will write a descriptive narrative. Both input and output are considerations for addressing the learning styles of students.

As stated earlier, a one-size-fits-all approach to teaching does not work. All students are not the same in how they learn and how they best demonstrate their learning. In varying your presentation and providing options for students to complete and submit their projects and assignments, you help your students gain self-awareness about their preferences and strengths, and support them in setting goals for addressing their weaknesses in other learning styles. This is especially important as we prepare students for higher education where attention to differentiation and learning styles is less prominent. Guiding your students in reflective appraisal of their own learning styles will help them understand and address their own strengths and challenges.

As we close this chapter on high expectations and rigor in your social studies program, think about the rungs on the ladder of authentic learning. We spent time focused on the work that is required of you as an authentic teacher, and the work required of students as authentic, present, and engaged learners. The next chapter keeps us on these two rungs as we continue exploring the challenges and opportunities in the work and in our students. Here is a story that seems to address both as I reflect on my own journey as an authentic educator.

If you are like me, you are continually learning from your students. Let me tell you about an incredible student I had the honor to teach and learn from when he was in fifth and sixth grade. Andy was an interesting student who was clearly uncomfortable with his growth spurt and onset of preadolescence. He was highly intelligent, had a great sense of humor though rarely smiled, and seemed to have few friends. He pretended like school was the worst thing to happen in his life, and he responded to every assignment by saying it was "dumb." His mother was a middle school teacher and expected him to behave, get good grades, and not cause any trouble for me or our class. She insisted on frequent meetings to make sure her son was doing his work and not causing any problems.

I realized that Andy needed to have roles and responsibilities in our classroom and during small group projects that were unique and suited to his disposition. I had no doubt that he was learning the material and could do the work assigned (although he often resisted doing the actual work). One day after school, Andy's mother came to visit me and check up on her son. She looked around the room and saw colorful works of art created by students studying about life underwater. Using paper plates, students illustrated, painted, and added materials to their underwater scenes to make 3D portholes covered by plastic wrap to simulate the glass window in a submarine. Andy's mother spotted his porthole right away and started to apologize. She asked me to take down his artwork because she said it was embarrassing. She stared at the paper plate covered completely by black marker. I explained to her that I had asked Andy to explain his underwater scene, which was quite a departure from those created by his classmates. He launched into a story about the submarine going to the depths of the ocean where sunlight could not reach the life that existed there in darkness. He spun a tale of mystery and intrigue that made me wonder what might be lurking at such depths of the ocean (and his imagination). It was my favorite porthole in the entire classroom!

Andy reminded me time and time again not to promote conformity in my classroom. He learned that our classroom was a place for him to be himself. It was also a place where creativity and individuality were honored and celebrated. I am sure that he inspired risk-taking and creativity in his classmates too. He also taught me to take the time to ask questions of students about their work rather than making assumptions and hasty decisions in order to get the grades done. There was so much more to assess about his work and the work of other students when I took the time to probe and listen to students' reflective responses about their own work.

Don't get me wrong—I still had to push Andy to produce work, complete assignments, and recognize that learning was not "dumb." I was thrilled to have fifth-grade Andy return to my class the following year for sixth grade. And when he left for middle school, I found a typewritten note on my desk. Andy knew I had a passion for old typewriters. The note read, "In the words of Charlie Chaplin, 'Anyone can make a person cry. It takes a genius to make a person laugh.' And you, Miss Schell, make me laugh. Love, Andy."

See? I can be fun too!

SECTION 3

AUTHENTIC CLASSROOMS

Chapter 4

From Goals to Grades

"Being in your element is not only about aptitude, it's about passion: it is about loving what you do . . . tapping into your natural energy and your most authentic self."
—Sir Ken Robinson

If you are familiar with the late, great Sir Ken Robinson, you know that he challenges all educators to reconsider the ways in which students learn in schools today. His 2010 video titled "Changing Education Paradigms" has been viewed nearly 17 million times, gaining global attention and causing educators to wonder about their practice. The video carries the simple yet powerful message that times have changed and therefore schools must change to reflect the current world in which we live. Continuing to organize studies and provide incentives for learning that reflect the Enlightenment period and industrial era makes little sense in the 21st century. While we may not be able to immediately do away with bell systems, subjects presented in silos, brick-and-mortar learning environments, and a school calendar that confounds most people, teachers can make a big difference in their classrooms to impact learning that makes sense in this day and age. And they can find better ways to connect with their students to inspire learning that yields more than stickers, grades, or the promise of a "good job."

We can begin with motivation—for students learning and for teachers teaching.

What drew you into the field of education? My guess is that you had a passion for teaching or for the subject(s) that you teach. Perhaps you were inspired by a favorite teacher while you were a student or a family member who also served as a teacher. Your personal motivation for teaching may have morphed or shifted during your years in the profession, but there is a compelling reason for you to get out of bed each morning, rack your brain for solutions to the challenges presented by students and lessons, and work tirelessly to provide feedback to students based on their work and progress in your class. Without this source of motivation, you would probably not remain in the classroom—especially at this time when we are experiencing the "great resignation" and seeing a lot of educators leave their jobs for various reasons.

In order for you to bring your authentic self into your classroom each day, you must maintain a clear connection to that source of motivation that brought you into teaching and that sustains you to this day. I know how easily we can lose touch with our passion and purpose because of the incredible demands on every teacher. Keeping that flame alive and within sight has been especially difficult in recent years as political divisions have grown wider and more heated, racial justice issues have generated mass protests worldwide, climate change has caused devastation locally and globally, and the COVID-19 pandemic has affected every aspect of our lives. We are living during a time of social, economic, and environmental reckoning, which is both exhausting and exhilarating. Change is a constant in life that demands our attention and response. To best navigate these unprecedented changes and stay the course as teachers, it is essential that educators hold firm to their source of inspiration and grounding. It is important for teachers to identify, clarify, and understand their purpose. Then, changes can be made to adapt to new curriculum, policies, initiatives, assessments, leadership, and protocols without losing yourself as a teacher who entered the profession with a clear purpose in mind.

Students are particularly clever in spotting teachers who are grounded, authentic, and committed to student learning. On the flip side, they are also very good at identifying (and toying with) teachers who are unsure, untethered, and lack confidence in their purpose. So, if necessary, track down and dust off that philosophy of education statement that you were required to write in your preservice education program or recall the values and commitment that brought you into the teaching profession. Rewrite your philosophy statement. Make yourself an infographic or artistic rendering. Revisit, reevaluate if necessary, and strengthen your resolve as an educator so that this becomes apparent to your students and provides you with the clarity necessary when making decisions inside and outside of the classroom. Let your authentic teaching self-serve as your core and as a source of motivation for all that you do.

At the same time, we have all experienced a great deal during the COVID-19 pandemic, racial unrest, economic and political upheaval, and climate disasters. We can neither forget nor ignore what has impacted us individually and collectively. Paying attention to the lessons learned during these unprecedented times, we can bring forward our passion and purpose with greater compassion and understanding for students and families who experience loss, despair, discrimination, homelessness, hunger, stress, and trauma. As we have experienced shifts in our own priorities to protect our health and safety, teachers should have greater empathy for students whose priorities do not include homework and social studies because they are suffering from challenges to their mental health and well-being.

As stated in the beginning of this book, one of the most challenging aspects of teaching social studies is student engagement. How do you motivate students to dive into their studies of history, geography, economics, civics, and government? You might have some creative and successful hooks (or anticipatory sets) for lessons, such as:

- Displaying a cartoon strip to read, generate a laugh, and discuss informally with the class before beginning the lesson. Something about the cartoon might have a connection to the lesson, but perhaps not.
- Telling a joke or riddle for students to ponder and guess the answer.
- Playing music from the culture, region, or era that students are studying in the lesson.
- Brainstorming what students know or think about a term, historical character, group of people, location, or concept that leads into the lesson.
- Presenting a news item to discuss with some connection or alignment to the lesson (e.g., immigration issues in the news connected to studies of immigration, Supreme Court rulings related to studies of the Constitution, archaeological finds aligned with studies of prehistoric or ancient cultures, etc.).

Those hooks might be good for gaining students' attention and leading them into a lesson, but how does this keep them engaged in the larger goals that you have for them as social studies students? Do these techniques help students to see the real-world value of their studies with consistency and enhance personal connections to their learning? If so, keep doing them. If not, reconsider what might truly motivate your students to take seriously their studies of how the world works in places near and far, during times past and present, and with cultural values that are familiar and foreign.

For decades, we have used stickers, points, grades, test scores, and college entrance requirements to motivate students in our social studies classrooms. "You want to get a good job, don't you?" echoes up and down the hallways of high schools. In doing so, we have assumed that students are motivated by grades, care about their test scores (on classroom assessments, Advanced Placement exams, or standardized tests), and see college as something in their future. These assumptions might be correct for some students, but probably not for all students. While grades, tests, and college entrance requirements may continue to exist and serve some students, how might we shift our emphasis on these factors to provide motivation for all students in our classes? How can we help students to see the value in learning social studies as beneficial to everyone?

So what motivates students to learn social studies? First of all, I refuse to believe that any student comes to school on any given day determined to fail at their education. Many have issues and circumstances that get in the way of rising to the standards and expectations that we place before them, and many simply do not value grades and test scores. As presented in Chapter 1, teachers can find out what motivates students by asking them what is important and of interest to them. Asking students to be self-reflective about what makes them want to learn is an excellent exercise that can inform you in your instructional design. The key here is to pay attention to what students share with you and use that information in ways that demonstrate appreciation and respect for their insights and differences. I have seen some teachers ask for personal information only to use it against students or in ways that made the students wish they never opened up in the first place. That should never happen.

What is important to your students? What interests them? If your students take the invitation seriously, chances are they will share some versions of:

- I care about my friends and my family.
- I want to find out what I am good at.
- I have so many questions and want to figure things out.
- I really do want to do well in school.
- I do not want to look dumb to anyone.
- I want to have a good life (make money, have things, gain access to opportunities).
- I want to do something good.
- I want to be happy and not bored.

While these responses may not seem closely connected to your social studies content, you can learn a lot about each student who responds and find patterns across groups of students. If these were the responses from my students, I would see connections to lessons about:

- Relationships and family structures
- Exploration, ambition, skills, innovation, workforce
- Cultural universals, natural and human systems, history, geography
- Education, rules and laws, civic engagement
- Social mores and interactions, multiple perspectives, culture

- Economics, religion, philosophy, sociology, civics, human rights
- Common good, civic engagement, social responsibility, cultural values

These are lessons spread throughout social studies and offer opportunities to connect with students with examples, challenges, and characteristics of what they also find important in their lives. If students are able to see the intersections between social studies content and their personal journeys in life, they will value their lessons and develop internal motivation that sustains them in continuing to learn about people and events, systems and structures, policies and practices, and places. At the same time, help them recognize the important skills they learn and develop in social studies, including:

- asking questions
- organizing information
- separating facts from fiction or opinions
- weighing costs and benefits
- critical thinking and decision-making
- using context to understand
- recognizing multiple perspectives and cultural influences
- active listening
- keeping an open mind
- systems thinking
- leadership

Students should be aware of your goals for teaching social studies, and they should be guided in developing their own goals for learning the subject. When they have clear goals, they are better able to monitor their own progress and hold discussions with you and others about how they are doing in social studies. As a social studies teacher, I had goals that looked something like this:

> Students will understand that the stories of the past inform who we are and how we live today. They will explore their own communities and cultural heritage as well as cultural elements from others while learning that (in the United States) we live in a diverse democracy consisting of people from different backgrounds and identities. Students will learn how people rely on the land and natural resources to sustain life and build productive economies. They will investigate systems created to bring about order in local, national, and global communities.

In my classes, students used journals to keep their notes, questions, and responses to prompts presented in class. At the front of the journal were goals that they created at the beginning of the year and revisited when it was a good time for reflection—at the end of a unit, before grading periods, when they were struggling to remember why social studies was important, etc. When I met with individual students, I often asked them to refer to the front of their journals to discuss their goals and progress they were making toward those goals. Sometimes, students wanted or needed to revise their goals, which was a perfectly healthy exercise. We all need to be reminded of our goals and why we are either working so hard or to nudge us into a direction requiring us to work a bit harder or smarter. Student's goals looked something like this:

Elementary

- I will read for information before I ask questions.
- I want to learn how to read maps and make them too.
- I will figure out why people fought to have their land.
- I want to know what happened to Native Americans.
- I will learn the history of California.
- I want to learn how money works.
- I will learn new terms to use when I tell people what I am learning.
- I want to learn interesting stories.

Secondary

- I will learn my roles and responsibilities as a US citizen.
- I will learn from different people's accounts about what happened in history.
- I will make a map of the world.
- I will ask a lot of questions about what we are learning.
- I will find out what ordinary people were doing in history.
- I want to find out what makes people famous.
- I want to understand what is meant by the common good.

Some goals related to knowledge building and others related to practices or skills to be developed. Students were able to develop their own goals so they could start where they felt most comfortable as students of social studies and determine where they wanted to go in their education. I watched some students completely forget about their goals as others took them seriously, achieved them, and continued to set new goals during the year. This allowed students to have greater voice and control of their own learning, and allowed me to guide and support students in ways that were meaningful to them. I would also like to think that students continued to set personal and academic goals for themselves beyond my social studies class. When I shared with them some of my life goals (e.g., running a 10K, buying a house, raising a son who respected himself, others, and the environment), I did so to provide examples of how goal-setting is useful, practical, and authentic.

Setting, reviewing, and revising goals allows both teachers and students to continuously monitor their progress in social studies. This also helps to break away from the misconception that the subject is a collection of disconnected units of instruction. For example, I have been in sixth-grade classrooms where students were learning about early humans and ancient civilizations. For each civilization, the teacher had a separate bin to hold the readings, realia, simulation materials, etc. When students were done learning about Egypt or India, they literally packed up the bin and moved on to the next bin to learn about China or Greece. While this organizational structure is helpful in many ways, it requires "connective tissue" to help students recognize the common and unique features across these civilizations. In many cases, completing a unit in the textbook can yield the same results—introduction to the topic or event, immersion, test/project, done. Restart the cycle with the next unit in the book. Continuous monitoring of goals can help students to understand the currents that run throughout social studies as opposed to setting goals specific to a unit that tend to focus on the content of that unit.

To help students with self-reflection, they should be guided to analyze the evidence that helped them to determine their own progress. I had a student who wanted to push herself to ask more questions in class because she wanted to stay engaged in class discussions and felt like she tuned out when she felt "lost" and unsure about the material. With her goal of asking more questions, I suggested that she keep tally marks in her notebook to document each time she asked a question in class. When we met to monitor her progress, she referred to the times she felt more confident and up-to-speed by pointing to the tally marks at the top of her notes. Conversely, she expressed confusion about some of the lessons and when we looked for tally marks in her notes, we found few or none. Working with students to monitor their learning was far more effective than what I did in my earliest days of teaching when I took piles of student work home to evaluate on my own, added grades to my grade book, and handed back papers to students with marks and grades before moving on. Students learning and practicing strategies for addressing challenges is something I want them to do well beyond my social studies class and their school experience. If they can develop a mindset and habits to embrace—rather than avoid or succumb to—opportunities in life, I feel I have done my job as an educator.

How do you help your students to monitor their work and progress in your class? Rather than just announcing assignments and collecting work by a due date, think about the multiple opportunities for checking in with students between those two events. Monitoring progress can happen within a project or across assignments. Make plans to create a manageable system that allows you to help each student monitor their progress in your class. This could mean collecting reflection journals from half or one-third of the class each week for review and feedback—alternating the next week. Or, setting up conferences with students or table groups that alternate across the days and weeks. Note of caution: One year I allowed students to sign up for time slots to conference with me and I advised them to schedule a conference at least once every two to three weeks. Most students organized their agendas to do exactly that. However, some were noticeably missing from my conference schedule. While I wanted them to take responsibility and ownership of their progress, which included conference sessions with me, some needed me to intervene and assign conferences for them.

Finally, let's take a look at mastery of learning or evaluation of student work. These are two different concepts that should converge as we assess student work as evidence of learning. In evaluating the student work, we should be able to determine to what degree each student has mastered the learning targets for that assigned work. Ideally, the work produced provides information to both student and teacher related to those learning targets. I used to explain to my students that learning is covert, or not clearly seen on the outside; hidden. I told them that what they produce makes their learning overt, or observable, outside of their minds; revealed. Using this explanation and reminding students that my job was to report out their observable learning of the standards, I was then able to help them focus on our learning targets. This helped all of us from taking too many bird walks in our lessons and in their work.

Yes, we would all take bird walks because everything is connected and everything is interesting or important. However, our focus was clearly articulated in our standards and on their standards-based rubrics and report cards. These became helpful as students tended to spend more time and attention on making their work attractive—playing with fonts and images/clips for multimedia presentations or adding more color and glitter to the cover of a report or project. I acknowledged the value of those elements of their work, but pointed to the purpose of the assignment to reiterate and refocus. When helpful, I would share a mini lesson on advertisement and propaganda techniques that draw the person's attention away from costs, dangers, and other important information causing the reader to be influenced without having all of the facts. I told students that my job is to look beyond the glitter and fancy fonts in order to determine what they actually learned and how they used that learning to present their project.

We work in a system that assigns grades or determines proficiency in meeting established standards. Those grades and marks are decided in the evaluation of student work using a performance rubric, point scoring guide, or grade/marking system. In all cases, it is most important that students understand how their work is being assessed. And, it is helpful for them to know what this number, letter, or marking means for them as a student in your social studies class. Long gone are the days of "gotcha" or using assessments as a form of punishment. I remember some of my teachers in both elementary and secondary grades "threatening" us with pop quizzes, difficult exams, and additional work assignments if we did not improve our behavior. If we want to assess student learning against specific goals, objectives, standards, and targets, we must separate classroom management from student assessments.

Additionally, assignments that generate student work must align with specific standards—content and skills—or learning goals and objectives. Student work should be engaging and meaningful in response to compelling or essential questions that frame their learning. Offering choice and voice in those assignments will enhance student engagement as they decide whether they can best respond to the prompt through writing, multimedia, performance, or a physical model. This is one way to differentiate your assessments if the assignment can be accomplished in these or other ways. There will be times when you do need every student to write an essay or draw a map or complete a timeline. Just make sure that the assignment and evaluation align with the learning focus. Including broader knowledge or skills development in a rubric is necessary in some assignments, but should be made clear to students.

For example, if students are learning about the Age of Exploration/Discovery, their unit assessment might require them to compare and contrast exploration from the 15th–18th centuries with exploration in the 21st century. Students might be given a choice between writing a 3–5 page essay or narrating a 10-minute multimedia presentation. The rubric would include criteria that is stated in the standard(s) guiding this unit, such as tracing exploration routes, describing the characteristics of explorers, and explaining early navigational tools. Additional criteria might relate to long-term learning goals, such as conducting cost-benefit analyses, chronological thinking, or identifying cause and effect.

In evaluating student work and setting mastery as a goal, consider what might help students to reach for that goal. If they don't understand or care about mastery of social studies learning goals, they will either go through the motions to get the assignment done with little investment or they will avoid the assignment altogether. This is where your passion for history and the social sciences comes shining through in your classroom. Help your students to consider the importance of historic events, human and technological progress, geographic and environmental perspectives, economic reasoning, law and order, etc.

Analogies, metaphors, current events, music, art, and other tools can help you connect your students with the content and purpose for evaluation.

If appropriate, let your students negotiate mastery and evaluation criteria. Student-generated rubrics are powerful tools in themselves, but also benefit students through the process of determining what criteria is necessary to evaluate learning. Oftentimes, we define high-quality work with some bias based on our skills and experiences. For many social studies teachers, writing essays, reports, and multiple choice tests are the standard for evaluation. Talk with your students about alternative forms of making their learning overt. I can tell you that oftentimes writing a succinct and precise tweet with a limited number of characters is far more challenging than writing a page of narrative text. (I learned this when I worked as an editor for the children's newspaper *Weekly Reader*. I was limited in the number and kinds of words I used to write news articles about serious issues, such as elephant poaching or gun control laws, for young readers. That was challenging!) To get to the heart of learning, sometimes less is more. And at times, we want students to use their creative and hands-on abilities to demonstrate their learning in ways that are reflected in the real world. Why not demonstrate student learning through:

- a museum exhibit
- a website
- filmed interviews
- children's picture books
- poetry
- music
- dramatic performance
- sculpture or mural

- a magazine, newspaper, brochure, or newsletter
- scored discussion
- teaching corners (students teaching others)

One last note about student work is this: Revision has value. I think we can all remember a time in our lives when we learned important lessons by having to revise or redo something. Whether a recipe or meal, drawing or painting, or letter or report, we learned to go back and try again. We thought we could cut corners or make our own adjustments in the process, and later realized that the results really needed our full attention and precision. Not all things in life—or all social studies assignments—require revision. However, many things do. We can identify our own reasons for why we want to put forward our best work and take full advantage of the learning process. We can help our students find their own reasons too. Some of those reasons just might bring them back to their goals.

SECTION 3: AUTHENTIC CLASSROOMS

Chapter 5
Teaching What Matters

"Real education should educate us out of self into something far finer; into a selflessness which links us with all humanity."

—Nancy Astor

How can we help students to view social studies as more than a string of events, a cast of historical characters, and information plotted on a bunch of maps? Maybe you, too, have heard students describe history as "one damned thing after another." The quote is actually attributed to a historian dating back to the 1950s who is said to be influenced by an even earlier quote stating that "life is one damned thing after another." However the story goes, I am surprised to learn about the longevity of this phrase and I take comfort in seeing the connection between history and life. History is, indeed, about life's past events as they relate to people and places. However, I do not want students to feel as though they are trapped in a never-ending soap opera.

At any grade level and especially across grade spans, an analysis of the content that students are expected to learn in social studies is overwhelming. Daunting. Challenging. Years ago, we called social studies a "march through time" as teachers set the course at the beginning of the year and instructed students to "keep up." Any disruption to the quick pace that was established would mean falling behind, and that was especially disconcerting if the class was Advanced Placement or International Baccalaureate. If there was an end-of-course exam or state assessment in social studies, this fast pace and wide coverage was on every teacher's mind. In some states, educators counted the number of standards required of students at each grade level and used this large quantity to raise concerns about quality teaching and learning. The evolution of "power standards" or priority standards challenged educators to identify and teach the essential or most important content in their standards to alleviate this burden. The concept of essential standards reemerged recently as educators tried to address the loss of learning due to the COVID-19 pandemic. Do you feel comfortable deciding which content is more important for students to learn and therefore what gets compressed or eliminated in your course? My guess is that your answer is "no." However, isn't this what teachers are faced with every day in planning and teaching social studies lessons?

Given the finite number of hours that you have to teach social studies and the imprecise science of student comprehension, choices must be made throughout the instructional planning process. Even when you determine approximately how many weeks to spend on instructional units, some classes will require additional time due to limited background knowledge, poor skills development, or another challenge identified by paying attention to your students during the learning process.

How can we help students to make sense of all those standards, units, chapters, and expectations for learning in your social studies class? Some teachers start at the beginning of the textbook or curriculum and try to get as far as possible. Sometimes this leads to learning and oftentimes it does not.

To help students make sense of the abundance of information presented in a typical social studies class, teachers can identify the topics under which these facts and skills are presented. When students have a general idea how information is organized, they find greater success in learning the content. Consider how schema is built as students create "placeholders" in their brains for information. Topics, such as headings or categories, help students to find information and make sense of the details. For example, students learning about US symbols in the early grades learn that the national flag, Statue of Liberty, and bald eagle symbolize American history, culture, geography, and values. Older students might study topics such as the Civil War, immigration, or women's rights. While learning about these events and issues, those details fall under one topic or another.

Topics can also be presented as concepts. Concepts provide a broader view of events, issues, eras, cultures, and places by providing multiple examples for students to study. For example, young students might study about leadership as a concept and learn about President Abraham Lincoln, Dr. Martin Luther King Jr., Marie Curie, and Malala Yousafzai as leaders. As they learn about these historical figures and their accomplishments as leaders, students are also learning about the characteristics of leadership. They can discuss how leaders work in different fields, come from different backgrounds, and lead in different ways. Students explore leaders in their own lives—at school, at home, in their communities, in their country, and around the world. Students might not recall every detail from their studies of leaders, but they leave this unit with a better understanding of leadership and carry that conceptual lens into subsequent studies and their lives. Additional concepts for young learners include citizenship, family, community, and culture.

For older students, they might study concepts of justice, revolution, legacy, authority, conflict, genocide, innovation, or interdependence. Some instructional units lend themselves to certain concepts, such as power while studying imperialism. Or independence during studies of the American Revolution or framing a new nation. Diffusion is a concept that ties together studies of global trade and the Age of Exploration. Older students are able to identify examples of these concepts that play out in their personal lives and in the news. They can connect previously studied material to concepts, too, which helps them to see commonalities across people living across time and space.

Similar to concepts, themes are frequently used in social studies to help students make sense of a lot of material presented within or across chapters and units. The National Council for the social studies organized national social studies standards (1994) under these ten themes:

- Culture
- Time, Continuity, & Change
- People, Places, & Environments
- Individual Development & Identity
- Individuals, Groups, & Institutions
- Power, Authority, & Governance
- Production, Distribution, & Consumption
- Science, Technology, & Society
- Global Connections
- Civic Ideals & Practices

Similarly, the California History-Social Science Framework (2016) introduced these seven key themes for K–12 teachers to consider in their instructional design:

- Patterns of Population
- Uses and Abuses of Power
- Worlds of Exchange
- Haves and Have-Nots
- Expressing Identity
- Science, Technology and the Environment
- Spiritual Life and Moral Codes

Themes like these allow for students to compare and contrast topical examples presented in the formal curriculum with additional examples highlighted by students or teachers. These themes are also relevant to students' lives, families, and communities. Effective teaching and learning with themes provides students with interconnected views of the world—past and present—and allows them to consider the opportunities and challenges as well as the conditions and choices for human beings throughout time. With compelling themes, students continue their own investigations of the world as they build relationships, take perspectives, pursue higher education, and make decisions about their careers and future.

Just as National History Day presents a new theme each year for students to conduct historical research and present an exhibit, documentary, performance, or essay on a topic under that theme, think about what inviting and exciting themes might frame your units, semesters, or entire school year. Here are some examples of History Day themes from years past:

- Conflict and Compromise in History
- Turning Points in History
- Triumph and Tragedy in History
- Exploration, Encounter, Exchange in History
- Frontiers in History
- Revolution, Reaction, Reform in History

Some teachers prefer to organize their course content around Big Ideas or Essential Questions as introduced by Jay McTighe and Grant Wiggins in their work presented as *Understanding by Design* (1998). Whether presented as statements or questions, these enduring understandings are defined as important, engaging, thought-provoking, and transferable within, across, and beyond the curriculum. Essentially, these statements or questions get to the "why" of social studies and help our students recognize the relevance of learning history, economics, geography, and civics and government. Here are some examples to consider or use as models for the Big Ideas or Essential Questions that you might use in your class:

Big Ideas
- Where people live influences how they live.
- People move to improve their lives or because they are forced.
- All communities have a history.
- People, ideas, events, and eras shape history.
- Limited resources require choices.
- Rights have limits.

Essential Questions
- What is a global citizen?
- What are people willing to fight for?
- How does the environment affect people?

- What is the value of a government?
- How do new ideas cause change?
- Why do borders exist?

Thinking back to our ladder metaphor, teachers are consistently making choices, decisions, and changes related to their social studies curriculum based on their capacity, student engagement, available curriculum and resources, and what is happening in the world—locally and globally. When you organize the lessons and details of your lessons under topics, themes, concepts, or enduring understandings (Big Ideas or Essential Questions), those decisions and changes can become more manageable. In this age of searching up facts and connected information on the Internet, students know they can find information at their fingertips and therefore invest less in classroom studies. However, they do know that there are skills required to do that online research, including knowing what types of questions to ask before fact-finding. Therefore, today's students will benefit from learning useful topics, concepts, and themes that are relatable and intriguing. Teaching with these can allow students to access, use, and value their lived experiences that provide insights into how the world works. That is a powerful way to engage students in social studies while helping them prepare for citizenship, leadership, and exploration.

SECTION 3: AUTHENTIC CLASSROOMS

Chapter 6
Independent, Collaborative, and Relevant Work

"Authenticity is a collection of choices that we have to make every day. It's about the choice to show up and be real. The choice to let our true selves be seen."
—Brene Brown

How did you learn social studies when you were in school? What did you do with the information presented in your classes? In what ways did you practice and develop the skills of social studies? How did you use the tools of the discipline?

These are all important questions to consider as you reflect on your own formative experiences as a student of social studies. For some people, remembering their social studies classes might present a challenge—especially if the experiences were not enjoyable or particularly memorable. In this case, teachers should be inspired to seek out engaging and meaningful instructional practices and resources for their students. Social studies *should* be an enjoyable class with engaging content that relates to the students and helps them understand their world—locally as well as globally. Social studies lessons *should* make for memorable learning experiences because students are invested in their learning. Ideally they are left with even more questions about themselves, others, and how the world works than they had when they entered the lesson. Social studies *should* create the desire to learn more while students are practicing the skills of inquiry, critical thinking, economic reasoning, spatial analysis, and civic engagement.

For others, these memories might be overwhelmingly positive and, in fact, a motivating factor for becoming a social studies teacher. Reflecting on what made this discipline so inviting, interesting, and memorable—whether the content, learning activities, or teacher—is an important exercise while keeping in mind that not all students have the same positive response and experiences with social studies content, learning activities, or teachers. Teachers who found social studies interesting and engaging as students should consider their positionality, or how their identity provides access to information and opportunities, in terms of the curriculum and learning environment. To achieve the goal of providing access and meaningful learning opportunities for all students, we must all look beyond our own educational experiences. Our students are typically very good about sharing their opinions and experiences in learning history, geography, economics, and civics/government.

All social studies teachers should think deeply about the work, or learning experiences, that students are expected to do in their class each day and throughout the course. This chapter takes into consideration the value and roles of independent work, collaboration, and relevance. We know that students have personal learning styles and preferences that enhance their abilities to learn, apply, reflect, and evaluate. Many students will self-identify as learners: visual, kinesthetic, or auditory; hands-on, reader, or observer; fast or slow; independent or team-oriented. Some have internalized character trait or personality profile results and will tell you their strongest and weakest intelligences among interpersonal, intrapersonal, spatial, linguistic, logical/ mathematical, musical, bodily-kinesthetic, and naturalist; affinity for thinking, feeling, intuition, and sensing; social-emotional capacities for relationship-building, decision-making, and self-reflection. And some students will flat-out tell you that they are "not good at social studies" or "not good at school." Taking all of this into consideration while aware of our own personal learning experiences, let's explore how to center students in the classroom to achieve authenticity through their work.

Remember our ladder? Consider "work" as one of the rungs on that ladder for authentic learning. You might feel prepared for the lesson content and learning context. What about the work that you expect from our students? Does it align with the learning goals and promote authentic learning for everyone in your class? Keeping in mind the cognitive demands and skill levels required for the work, are there opportunities for all students to succeed in their learning through independent work or collaborative work? And, what will motivate students to engage in the work?

Independent Work

When you were learning social studies, did you work independently? If so, there was probably a lot of reading, writing, and test-taking involved. Maybe there were projects that you were assigned to complete on your own—illustrating a timeline of historical events, making a map, or covering poster board with images, captions, and other forms of information. How much did these independent work assignments contribute to your social studies education? Did these learning activities help you build your knowledge base as well as your thinking and analytical skills?

Chances are we all experienced a good amount of independent work in our social studies classes. Traditional practices included an abundance of lecture, reading, writing, and answering questions. The addition of student projects, including construction of dioramas and models, posters and multimedia reports, oral history interviews, and character interpretation, allowed for more variety and interaction with the subject matter. For many teachers, they will tell you this "makes social studies fun." There is definitely a need and a place for fun in social studies education. And, these are all useful strategies for introducing students to new content and skills, helping them develop a sense of the disciplines, and allowing them to process information appropriately. However, these learning exercises remain solo endeavors designed for individual students to either extend their knowledge and skills beyond reading, listening, and writing or to replace lectures and readings with more engaging strategies. The acquisition of information, development of understanding, and practice of skills is conducted independently and repetitively across the classroom. Students are left to discover and figure things out on their own through assigned materials and activities. Ultimately, their work is examined and evaluated by the teacher.

For many students—particularly those with high levels of literacy and motivation—independent learning is successful. Students learn to navigate materials and projects with the assistance of their teacher and their classmates. In the end, both teacher and student become aware of the student's proficiencies with the course content. What about those students who cannot manage independent work effectively? They might show up as disinterested or disruptive. A deep analysis should reveal what those students need in order to find success with independent work (e.g., disciplinary literacy skills, understanding about and appreciation for the discipline, self-confidence, culturally relevant pedagogy, etc.). And the teacher should build in structured or scaffolded support to meet those needs as the learning continues.

Independent learning in a social studies classroom can be useful and productive. Various types of independent learning activities play an important role for all students. Teachers must consider the purpose for independent learning and remain cautious about how much learning time is allocated to independent work. Overall, what message might we convey to students about the true nature of history and the social sciences if we present social studies solely as independent work? We know that historians require colleagues to find and corroborate sources as they build and defend arguments about historical accounts. Geographers work in teams to gather and analyze geographic data, display information in visual representations, and conduct field studies related to their research interests. Economists, anthropologists, sociologists, political scientists, and others whose work requires the knowledge and skills presented in social studies courses may spend some time working independently, but certainly do not work alone. The work of students in a classroom should reflect this reality.

Another consideration is the timing of independent work. When, during lessons, do students have opportunities to discuss information and negotiate ideas critical to their understanding and success with assignments? Also, how much time is provided for students to work with their peers in order to remain on-track with their independent work? In our teacher preparation courses, we used to propose an organized, systematic approach to lesson planning that looked something like this:

- Anticipatory Set for engagement (5 minutes)
- Direct Instruction for input (15 minutes)
- Collaborative Exercises for students to discuss or work with input (5 minutes)
- Independent Learning for students to work on their own (25 minutes)
- Closure for wrap-up and homework assignments (5 minutes)

This was structured as a gradual release of responsibility model for a typical 55-minute period. It was also a response to disrupt the traditional class period that involved lecture or film with assigned homework for independent work. This neat organizational guide for lessons worked at times but not in most cases. It did not work when the anticipatory set revealed that students did not complete or understand the previous lesson's homework and were not prepared for the day's lesson. It did not work when the anticipatory set revealed assumptions made by the teacher about prior knowledge and experience as a setup for the lesson. It did not work when lectures or "input" was incomprehensible or ran over allocated time. It did not work when students could not transform direct instruction into the planned collaborative exercise. And it did not work when students sat idly during independent work time because they were not ready to proceed from the collaborative exercise into work on their own. Imagine how challenging homework was for those students who did not find success with independent work time in class.

There is no magic recipe to answer the questions about "when" and "how much time" for independent work. Teachers know the scope and complexities of their content, instructional objectives, and learning context. Some lessons will be best learned with independent work at the beginning while others are more appropriate with independent work in the end. Some lessons and classes will be most successful with more time allocated to independent work while others are better suited to less time. A healthy and balanced approach to independent work will help address the diverse learning styles and needs of students while also supporting the development of both independent and collaborative learning skills in all students.

Collaborative Work

How can students work collaboratively in a social studies class to enhance their learning and skills development? Many projects are best achieved by students working together and bringing different experiences, perspectives, and skills to the tasks. In the process, students identify and develop essential skills that are not otherwise practiced when working independently. For example, communication and cooperation are required when people work together. These skills are related to others used in independent work, such as time management and organization. While students might be well organized and adept at managing time when working alone, these skills may fail pairs or teams of students without effective and consistent communication as well as cooperation skills. Consider the importance of all of these skills in what we teach about people and events of the past, economic systems, government policies and practices, and geographic perspectives. These and other skills should be relatable to students as they recognize the importance of developing them for their personal, social, and professional aspirations.

Since the 1980s, cooperative learning strategies have become common practice in many social studies programs. From the Think-Pair-Share to the Four Corners learning activities, students work cooperatively to bring their ideas together and enhance learning for all. Cooperative learning structures can be brief and useful strategies that meet the goal of increased student-to-student interaction and talking time. Spencer and Laurie Kagan introduced a variety of research-based tools, called structures, that have simple instructions and can be used repeatedly across lessons to limit teacher talking time so that students can develop social skills in a constructive learning environment. For example:

- Think-Pair-Share: Students are given a prompt and instructed to think about their response. Students are then paired up to share their responses with each other. Finally, students participate in a whole class discussion sharing what they thought, shared, and heard from their partner during the paired discussions.
- Think-Pair-Square: Students are given a prompt and instructed to think about their response. Students are then paired up to share their responses with each other. Pairs of students are instructed to "square" with another pair of students to share what they thought, shared, and heard from their partners during the paired discussions.
- Four Corners: Four options are posted in the four corners of the classroom. Students are instructed to select the best option based on the given prompt. For example, students might be asked to select the most appropriate analogy for the Civil Rights Movement. In each corner is an image showing either a flowing river, a large tree with deep roots, a caged lion, or a wildfire. Students are then provided a discussion prompt or task (e.g., draw a mural, create an infographic, develop a performance, etc.) to

complete with each other in that corner. Each group shares with the whole class why they selected that option, what was discussed, or the task completed.

- Jigsaw: Students number off and complete the reading or task assigned to students with that number. For example, if there are four sections to a text, audio recording, or video, students number off 1 to 4. Number 1s read/listen/watch one section, number 2s read/listen/watch another section, and so on. Students then meet in groups of four composed of one person representing each number (each group will have a 1, 2, 3, and 4 participant). In the groups, students work together to share what they learned or work together on a task that requires each to share information from their assigned text, recording, or video. A set of primary sources could also be used for Jigsaw. The goal is for students to collaborate in piecing together their information in order to gain a bigger, broader understanding of the material.

Cooperative learning structures are helpful strategies that encourage peer-to-peer discussions, problem-solving, critical and creative thinking, and project planning. These strategies decrease the amount of teacher talk or lecture time and increase the amount of time dedicated to student thinking, talking, and activity. In the process, students can recognize different perspectives on the topic or material and work together to figure things out. They learn to pose questions, develop research skills, and draw conclusions together.

Beyond these daily strategies, students can engage in longer-term collaborative work in the social studies classroom. Working in pairs, triads, or small groups, students can take on project-based or problem-based learning (PBL), youth participatory action research (YPAR), and design thinking. These are all methods of inquiry that can help students to develop and pursue compelling questions related to the content being studied, gather and analyze evidence, draw conclusions or develop arguments, and then share or take action according to the findings. In the process, students develop their historical and social science skills in addition to literacy and social skills. Oftentimes, students generate new lines of inquiry while they are seeking answers to their initial questions and developing a project of sorts to demonstrate their learning and proposed solutions.

Let's take a look at three models for inquiry-driven, student-centered, collaborative work in a social studies classroom.

Project-Based Learning

Project-based learning is a popular methodology used with students to investigate answers to complex questions or solve real-world issues. Guided by a driving question, students work together in pairs or small teams to analyze sources of information provided by the teacher and found through research. Buck Institute for Education is a national leader in PBL and presents these key elements of high-quality PBL:

- Challenging Problem or Question
- Sustained Inquiry
- Student Voice and Choice
- Critique & Revision
- Public Product
- Reflection
- Authenticity

Typically, teachers provide mini lessons throughout the week or weeks of a PBL unit to address learning needs identified by students and teachers during the inquiry cycle. However, during most of the work time in class, students are collaborating to understand the problem, answer the driving question, and present an authentic response as a project that reaches a wider audience than the teacher and class. In creating a public product as a response to the driving question, student work can be displayed in a school or district showcase or in a local coffee shop, community space, library or museum, or online. Student projects might result in campaigns to raise awareness, changes to policies and practices, or new programs in a community. Whether project-based or problem-based (starting with a problem), PBL helps students to connect their studies and skills development in social studies with real-world people, events, conditions, policies, and issues. With teacher guidance, students lead their planning, research, and project development. Students emerge with a variety of lessons learned—about themselves, their classmates, and their communities—in addition to the content determined at the beginning of the instructional unit.

Design Thinking

Design thinking provides opportunities for students to collaborate on issues that are meaningful to them and others. The process begins by identifying an issue related to the content studied in class and then seeking more information about the issue by empathizing with those who are directly affected by the issue. Students might read or listen to various accounts or conduct interviews to gain a better understanding of the issue from different perspectives. After learning about and from others, students work together to define the issue more closely. They might conduct a root cause analysis of the issue to clarify the problem, its roots, and its results.

After spending a good amount of time choosing an issue, empathizing with those impacted by the issue, and defining a problem that exists within the issue, students begin an iterative process of brainstorming solutions for the problem, selecting a solution from the options and creating a prototype, and then testing the prototype. Taking the proposed solution in prototype form back to the people directly affected by the issue is an important step in this process. Students learn quickly that oftentimes we generate solutions that either miss the mark or create even more problems due to unintended consequences. Based on the testing results, students might return to brainstorming, selecting and prototyping, and testing again. This cycle continues until the students are satisfied with a solution that holds up through testing to address the problem embedded in a larger issue. When they do, even more work ensues. Students create a plan for naming, funding, developing, and initiating or implementing their solution.

As students learn about human rights, environmental and social movements, immigration, democracy, housing and growth, employment, and other topics or themes, design thinking provides opportunities to see these same topics and issues in a local and contemporary context. Students build connections to people, practices, events, and policies of the past through their inquiry and perspective-taking. In the process, students see social studies as alive, evolving, and local as well as national and global.

Youth Participatory Action Research

YPAR is similar to design thinking and PBL, but driven primarily by students. Foundational to YPAR is the acknowledgment of the power in youth—their abilities and potential to investigate and determine actions necessary to address issues that are important to them, their families, and their communities. YPAR views power as shared between youth and adults in a dynamic process that focuses on teamwork, relationship-building, critical issues awareness, research, and advocacy or activism.

In all of these models, students wrestle with real-world issues that draw their attention and bring them into a cycle of inquiry. That cycle includes an important component of action, which ranges from changing personal behaviors to proposing policy changes in a community. The real value of using these methods in a social studies classroom is allowing students to better explore and investigate the world around them using their personal and cultural lenses on what matters. What draws their attention and encourages their data collection and analyses are the issues that affect their social, cultural, and economic lives. They are the issues within their environmental scope and require solutions that might be political or social in nature. Students see issues in ways that adults do not. They feel the weight and conflict of issues that might not be felt by adults. Providing students voice and choice in their projects and academic pursuits allows them to recognize their agency as individuals and as community members.

Like independent work, collaborative learning should not be the only method used in any classroom. Effective instruction and authentic learning requires a balance of independent and collaborative work. With each type, the appropriate teaching and practice of skills is also essential for student success. Some skills necessary for collaborative learning include active listening, contributions to group discussions and work, leadership, responsibility and accountability, sharing of resources, posing questions to support learning and progress, respect, and fairness.

Relevant Work

Students should know why they are doing work, or assignments, in your class. There are valid reasons for engaging students in work, but many might think that assignments are a waste of time or a form of punishment. Therefore, we must find ways to help students find value and relevance in their work.

For students of all ages, I find it helpful to discuss how we learn; how our brains process information and develop useful neural pathways. Brain research and learning theories introduced during the past two decades have expanded our understanding and appreciation for how we learn. I have seen teachers introduce these concepts to their students in ways that helped students realize the purpose of repetition (moving information from short-term memory to long-term memory), the value of organizing information (neural pathways and schema), utility of linguistics (where information is stored in the brain), and the importance of nutrition, exercise, and sleep (abilities to focus, maintain attention, retain and recall information). This information should not be kept secret from students. Many are self-aware and recognize the benefits of certain behaviors while some still attribute success or failure in school to disconnected factors or conditions (e.g., wearing a favorite T-shirt during a test, having a lucky pen, belief that this subject is not "for them," etc.).

In order to help students see the value in what they are

learning and how they are learning, we need to provide some insights into the decisions we make for student work in the social studies classroom. We are probably all familiar with the resistance that sparks in students when we make statements like "Do it because I said so" or "I'm the teacher and you are the student." So when instructing students, let them know the purpose of their assignments and entertain the questions they might have about the work. We need to help students see the relevance, or connectedness, in the work that they do. This can happen in different ways as students connect to lessons personally, through current context, and as they empathize with others.

Returning to some questions posed at the beginning of this chapter, reflect on these as you consider addressing relevance in student work in your classroom: *What did you do with the information presented in your classes? In what ways did you practice and develop the skills of social studies? How did you use the tools of the discipline?*

Whether or not you were guided to develop and use the information, skills, and tools of social studies in your own educational experience, you now have the opportunity to do so for your students. In determining the work to be completed for your course, ensure that students do something with the information they have learned. They can compare, contrast, unpack, connect, and generate new information or ideas or questions. Additionally, provide ways for students to practice using the skills embedded in social studies. They can create timelines, charts and graphs, maps, speeches, news reports, etc. Finally, there are tools of social studies that students can access and use to contribute to their work. At times, we have to add this as a requirement in the work (e.g., determine proximity of the settlement to the river using the map provided) and ultimately, we want students to be reaching for the tools they need in order to complete their work.

In real-world terms, think about how you plan for a road trip. There is information, there are skills, and there are tools that you require in order to successfully reach your destination. Students can benefit from the examples you share during lessons letting them know that their work will help them navigate museums and parks, estimate costs and make sound decisions about purchasing items and services, and determine appropriate questions and contexts when speaking with people or deciphering news reports.

SECTION 4

AUTHENTIC SOCIAL STUDIES

Chapter 7
Disciplinary Literacy

"Much of what students are asked to do in lessons (read, write, listen, speak, converse) is not authentic communication. They answer questions to make the teacher happy; they write essays that have the right features on the rubric to get as many points as possible; they tend to read texts just to get answers right on tasks and tests—actually, they often read the questions and then search for answers without reading the text completely."

—Jeff Zwiers

In the 1990s, a strong focus of our work in social studies was centered on literacy development. There was a reading crisis in our country and education leaders decided that we should increase "accountability" and concentrate efforts on teaching reading—across all disciplines. This was known as *reading in the content area* or *content area literacy*, and the slogan became "every teacher a reading teacher." The goal was to raise reading scores on state and national assessments at elementary, middle, and high school levels. With a strong literacy background, I embraced this challenge and paired up with my colleagues in English language arts to provide professional development aimed at adding explicit reading instruction to social studies.

As I started working with social studies teachers to integrate reading and writing strategies into their lessons,

I came to understand that there is a difference between learning to read and reading to learn. Educators drew a line in the sand to distinguish themselves as either a reading teacher or a teacher who uses reading and writing in their instructional program. I realized that while social studies teachers appreciate and use reading and writing in their classrooms, many are unprepared and unwilling to teach the skills of both—especially when faced with an already impacted curriculum. Additionally, we began to recognize that reading instruction in an English class is very different from reading instruction in a social studies class. Students needed to learn these different literacy strategies in order to make sense of the content presented in social studies classes, but where would they learn these different ways of comprehending and composing text? Social studies teachers had to step up.

Fast forward a couple of decades and we are still engaged in efforts to promote literacy development in social studies as seen in the Common Core State Standards for English Language Arts. These history/social studies standards align with other efforts to address disciplinary literacy in support of students' overall literacy skills development beyond the English classroom. When the Common Core State Standards were released in 2010, there was a buzz among social studies teachers who thought these English language arts standards replaced their social studies content standards—not so. There was also a flurry of English teachers who were concerned that their teaching must reflect the history/social studies content at their grade level, which was also not quite accurate. We began to see English teachers participating in professional development programs for social studies teachers, which was wonderful at the time. However, they soon learned that they were not going to be charged with teaching social studies content and skills after all with these new standards, and they stopped coming to our social studies workshops and meetings.

In the end, we all emerged with the realization that each discipline could support the other to best serve the academic achievement of students. It was interesting to see these concerns iron out over time with the understanding that we, as educators, should all communicate and work together across disciplines to truly support our students in both literacy development and disciplinary literacy as well as content learning.

What is Disciplinary Literacy?

With a focus on content area literacy, we learned that many social studies teachers had assumptions and expectations that students transfer their reading and writing skills from English lessons into social studies lessons and therefore did not explicitly teach students how to read primary and secondary sources, develop content vocabulary, and effectively build arguments in their writing assignments. Disciplinary literacy acknowledges that differences in literacy instruction do exist across the disciplines and therefore requires disciplinary teachers to learn what they are and how best to teach them to students.

We continue to learn and teach under the umbrella of disciplinary literacy in most social studies programs. Professional learning and curriculum materials reflect attention paid to the literacy development of students in social studies. Disciplinary literacy addresses what content area reading did not. As opposed to teaching reading strategies that apply to generic content, typically found in an English or language arts program, disciplinary literacy identifies the types of text and literacy skills used specifically in that discipline. In other words, the reading, writing, and ways of communication used specifically in that discipline. We know, for example, that maps are texts used often in social studies. We also know that reading maps requires specific knowledge and skills that differ from the knowledge and skills used in reading a poem presented in English, script used in drama, or equation introduced in mathematics.

A good way to introduce your students to disciplinary literacy is to ask:

- What types of text do historians use in their work?
- What types of text do geographers use in their work?
- What types of text are used in the field of politics and government?
- What types of text are used by those who work in fields requiring economic reasoning?
- How do historians and social scientists communicate with others in their work?
- When historians, geographers, and others who work in the social sciences produce work, what is the form or format used?

In other words, what do historians or geographers do—authentically—in their work? They work with and generate different types of "text" than professionals who work in other fields. What students read, write, and communicate in social studies classes should reflect what professionals read, write, and communicate in the real world. And their abilities to both read and produce these text types relies on explicit instruction found in disciplinary literacy lessons.

Students learning disciplinary literacy skills begin to understand that in social studies they may not find stories that have a beginning, middle, and end with an interesting cast of well-defined characters like they find in their English or drama classes. They learn to recognize the differences between literacy skills and text types in different disciplines. Ideally, they are learning the distinctions in disciplinary literacy across science, math, the arts, and so on.

As teachers and students consider questions like those above, they learn that individual historical records rarely articulate what we want and need to know about the event, place, or "main characters." Background information, context, and details are often lacking in any one source. The source may not provide information about what people were thinking or how their cultural values influenced their decisions. The source may be unclear about the connections and relationships between people, places, and events. Unlike a well-written novel, much of the "story" that we get in textbooks, films, and secondary source accounts is crafted through interpretation and corroboration of sources gathered and evaluated from a variety of places, including newspaper articles, private diaries, court records, speeches, letters, charts and maps, ledgers or logs, oral histories, photos, drawings, clothing, artifacts, songs, architectural records, books, advertisements, etc. The job of a historian is to piece together this information after using different tools and techniques for gathering, evaluating, and analyzing each piece. The assessment of each source type varies as well. For example, analyzing and interpreting a newspaper article requires a different approach than the analysis of a photograph. In efforts to uncover and understand the topic or issue under investigation, students will have to look for and decipher available sources while also inquiring about those not readily available in order to yield the best possible results. In the process, they will recognize that uncertainties prevail and that the work of historians, archaeologists, and anthropologists depends on accessible evidence and their abilities to "read" that evidence accurately.

Authentic, engaging social studies requires teachers to activate students' curiosity and interest in "decoding" the texts that are specific to this discipline. This can be done with some textbooks that include different text types, including maps, charts, graphs, photos, illustrations, speeches, diary entries, newspaper articles, other primary source excerpts, etc. Or, you can find and add various texts to supplement your textbook, which serves as a secondary source and requires its own attention to help students read with efficiency. Depending on the topics that you teach, you can also help students decipher cuneiforms, hieroglyphics, Sanskrit, characters, cave paintings, and other forms of text that are historical records. Whether I was teaching ancient world, early American, or California history, I included a variety of textual evidence, such as baskets, painted urns, buffalo robes, scrolls, and poetry carved into walls at Angel Island by Chinese immigrants. I wanted students to learn about the many ways people over time and place recorded their histories. I also wanted them to recognize that one person's story told in paint on a cave wall is just as important as another person's story told in an officially written and published document. Each text type required students to determine the format, author, audience, purpose, context, and message:

- What is this?
- Who created this?
- Who is the intended audience?
- Why was this created?
- What was happening at the time and in the place where this was created?
- What does this say?

While studying different text types to reveal messages from and about the past, I also enjoyed challenging my students to create their own historical records by writing journal entries, creating informational posters, designing brochures, and painting murals. By composing texts, they experienced the challenges and opportunities in various forms of text to communicate information. In the process, we discussed the differences in audience, interpretation, appreciation, utility, accessibility, and endurability of these different text types. Some formats allow for limited words to be used while others rely mostly on images to convey a message. Some are intended to speak to the general public while others are personal in nature. We talked about how inappropriate it felt to read other people's diaries and personal letters—even if they had died centuries ago. We also talked about what gets revealed in those diaries and letters, which may not be revealed in a published interview or public speech. Typically, this question arises when we discuss diaries, journals, or private papers: Who is the intended audience? The discussion is always fascinating, especially as I ask students who they are writing to in their own diaries or journals.

Ultimately, I would share with students my fascination with how people in the future will someday interpret our lives today. What will future generations think about our abundance of junk mail, advertisements, and campaign fliers? How will they decipher texts and digital documents stored on disks, hard drives, and in the cloud? What will they make of social media posts and podcasts? Will they have access to my bank information, credit card statements, and tax records? What do financial records, daily planners, magazines, websites, and photo albums have to say about me as an individual and society in general?

I wanted my students to become aware of the importance, influence, and impact of the many text types in their lives. They became better at noticing and reading billboards, posters, fliers, road signs, newspapers, newsletters, and food containers. And then they became good at separating fact from fiction in the texts we used in class and the texts they experienced in their real-world environments. They developed their sourcing abilities as they questioned who authored the text and why, when it was created and for what audience(s), and what purpose the text served. Of course, students also developed strong opinions about marketing and advertising, political campaigning, and wasted paper. They were immersed in disciplinary literacy skill development while also making important connections between social studies and their lives.

Students are learning that there are ways to read their social studies texts and the many sources introduced during their investigations. For most textbooks, students learn that features of the text include headings, subheadings, and narrative text. Within that text are terms that are presented in bold font or highlighted as vocabulary words—either academic vocabulary or content vocabulary—which help to name or classify information in an academic format. The text itself is primarily descriptive and sequential, using disciplinary concepts of chronology, cause and effect, and spatial and economic reasoning. Associated with the narrative text are different types of text that helps convey information in social studies, including images, political cartoons, maps, charts, graphs, and diagrams. Each example of text requires specific instructional support for how to read, or make sense of, the information presented. These lessons are helpful for student success in social studies across the grades, but also for success in understanding the text that helps us make sense of our world each day. News reports make use of maps, graphs, charts, and images to explain current events. Products and services typically come with directions or instructions. Most jobs require employees to read and follow manuals with procedures, regulations, and policies.

Today, most text is conveyed digitally through social media posts, text chats, email, websites, apps, and online authoring or multimedia tools. Print-rich environments have shifted from physical posters and billboards to displays on electronic devices. We can also help students to decipher these texts as they learn how to read their world. This can be done by guiding students to understand how technologies have fundamentally changed the ways that people connect and communicate information.

From the earliest days of sharing information, people communicated directly with each other using speech and motions. Prehistory is defined as the period of time before written records, but cave paintings and petroglyphs reveal some form of communication. History then tells us that records were kept and information shared using cuneiform, hieroglyphics, and other systems of writing. However, these texts were carved into clay, stone, or animal bones and painted onto papyrus or scrolls. These records were difficult to produce and transport, and with limited numbers of literate people, they were not plentiful or what we might call accessible. The invention of the printing press revolutionized communications and accelerated literacy in the world. I wonder if Johannes Gutenberg ever imagined the impact of the mass production of print on paper. A highly literate world then transferred from hard copy communications to digital form. With increased access to digital communications, we have experienced an explosion of available information. News stories that once required corroborating sources, fact-checking, and intense editing protocols have been overshadowed by instantly produced social media posts that go viral in a matter of minutes. Information sharing has changed so much that anyone with a device and connection can "report" events and make claims, which has led to the rise of misinformation, disinformation, and what some call "fake news." This is not to say that formal systems of reporting and communication from authorized agencies and organizations have not manipulated what they report, but in today's world of information gathering, one must use a critical lens to determine the source, context, audience, purpose, and message.

Media literacy is proposed in many school systems as a way to help students understand, manage, and discern messages delivered in various formats from different sources in today's digital age. These programs reiterate the fact that almost anyone can create content and, therefore, we should all be smart consumers of media, recognizing points of view, hidden agendas, and dangers posed through various platforms and messages. The skills presented in many media literacy lessons are aligned with disciplinary literacy lessons in social studies. Students learn to ask key questions, such as:

- Who created this?
- Why did they make it?
- Who is the message for?
- What techniques are being used to make this message credible or believable?
- What details were left out and why?
- How did the message make you feel?

(source: Common Sense Media)

Additional programs for digital literacy and digital citizenship provide lessons and information about online behaviors, how to evaluate a website, etiquette in digital spaces, and virtual exchange safety. Students have easy access to information, organizations, resources, and people who may not care about their safety, health, and welfare. In order to help them remain safe yet engaged in this world, we can bring authentic learning into our social studies classrooms through disciplinary and media literacy development while recognizing our students as digital natives.

Consider how you are helping your students to develop the literacy skills they need to be successful in your social studies class using the textbook or primary and secondary sources. Also, think about how the learning activities in your class mirror what professionals in social studies fields actually do for their work in history and the social sciences. Finally, connect with your students to determine how they are using and learning critical skills to manage and evaluate real-world literacy resources.

Chapter 8
Community-Based Projects

"Authenticity starts in the heart." —Brian D'Angelo

A school community is something very special. There is a tremendous amount of planning, work, organization, coordination, and effort that goes into making a school safe, inviting, and productive for the education of students over time. Each school community holds a unique history and shares a collection of stories representing success, disappointment, and change. Within school communities, students develop their knowledge and skills and showcase their learning. These displays of learning may appear as posters and artwork lining the windows and hallways to performances and exhibitions for peers. Sometimes, guests from outside the school community are invited inside for a look at what students are learning and producing within the school buildings. As a community volunteer, I must say that I always enjoy those invitations to learn from students.

Each school is also situated in a larger community. Communities are active with intersecting institutions, businesses, and agencies devoted to making things work. People strive to keep their communities safe, inviting, and productive too. For too long, educators have designated the teaching and learning of students to take place primarily on the school grounds. The exception, of course, has been homework and the occasional field trip.

Today, however, we are seeing a shift toward more community-based learning through school partnerships, projects, and internships. What could be more authentic than learning real-world skills in the real world in real time? Let's explore some rich and rewarding opportunities to recognize the context of learning for your social studies students and how that can impact their work in school while preparing them for future college and career decisions.

Partnerships

School and community partnerships are created for several reasons, and you should investigate the history and expectations for partnerships that exist with your school or district. Some schools form partnerships to provide connections to the local workforce, encourage good relations with city agencies and community-based organizations, generate a flock of volunteers to lend support in the classrooms or at school events, or strengthen ties between the school community and the greater community in which the school resides. In many cases, schools form partnerships with local colleges and universities to allow for student teachers and others in need of experiences in a K–12 education setting.

Whatever the reason for these partnerships, you should make yourself aware of what exists and what the terms are for those agreements. You might find there are none and choose to seek out partners to build authentic relationships for the benefit of your students. Why take these extra steps to reach outside of your school for support? As you think about making your social studies program more authentic for your students, consider the many ways that the subject plays out in your community—city workers, law enforcement, banking, commerce, transportation, public safety, representative leadership, cultural traditions and celebrations, health care, businesses, boundaries, landmarks, historic places, etc. There are real issues in your community too—pollution, theft, food insecurity, homelessness, vandalism, fires, accidents, etc.

Your local community is a place that students know well and want to learn more about. They may not understand why some roads are repaired while others are not, they may not know where their trash and recycling goes, or they may question the lack of green space available. They might wonder why they have to leave their community to purchase products or services, attend concerts or shows, or find a job. Students are already connected to their communities, they have a vested interest in where they live with their families, and the community offers multiple opportunities for research, investigation, and application of what they are learning in their social studies class. Most importantly, the community offers a real, genuine, authentic learning environment.

How might you utilize or form a partnership to enhance student learning in the real world of your local community?

Projects

If you are familiar with the Buck Institute for Education's gold standard for project-based learning, then you know that presenting projects to an authentic public audience is part of the criteria. I was so pleased to share this important aspect of projects with teachers who had not considered showcasing student work outside of the classroom or school. For far too long, students have been producing incredible work in a variety of formats that are only shared with the teacher and possibly with classmates. In those cases, the student effort was directed at the teacher whose obligation was to evaluate the work and assign a grade. What becomes of the project after receiving a grade? You can ask most custodians that question.

Remember the 35 toothpick bridges that I mentioned earlier in this book? Let me tell you the rest of that story. The teachers at this middle school were interested in project-based learning and shared those bridges as their students' first project. After a lot of professional development on project-based learning and *Understanding by Design* (McTighe & Wiggins), the teachers got to work. They identified their local community as a food desert and wanted their students to develop projects that helped them understand this issue, propose solutions in the community, and take action with their projects. The school Parent Teacher Association wanted to support these efforts and funded a greenhouse to be built on campus. The students created an aquaponics system in the greenhouse and grew butter lettuce and strawberries. Initially, the students planned to have a booth at the local farmer's market to talk with people about the importance of healthy foods in their community. They even planned to sell the produce from their greenhouse. However, the students also learned about the people in their community who could not afford access to fresh food even if it were available at the farmers' market. And so, the students changed their business plan—noting that there were too many profit-making enterprises in existence already—to a compassion plan and began distributing their produce free of charge to retirement homes, homeless shelters, and others in need.

These are the kinds of projects that make social studies teachers—all teachers—proud of their students and satisfied with the additional efforts required to go beyond the traditional instructional units. Stop and think about the implications of the lessons learned by these students who continue to live in this community and see the connections between what they are learning in school and what happens in the real world. These students remind me of the unheard voices in history—those who did not lead revolutions or build skyscrapers, but attended to the most vulnerable in society. These are the lessons about humanity that need to seep into our social studies programs.

In another example, let me introduce you to a group of ninth-grade geography students who were learning about global issues through the United Nations Sustainable Development Goals. Their teacher introduced them to design thinking and challenged them to identify an issue of personal, local, or global significance. The issues identified by students ranged from water pollution to human rights for immigrants; human trafficking for palm oil production to feminine hygiene product access; and fast fashion to environmental problems with refrigerants.

Students set out in pairs or individually to conduct empathy interviews from stakeholders in the community who were closest to the issue. One pair of students were investigating gender inequality in politics for their project and were encouraged by their teacher to call their city mayor for an interview – something they did not think they were allowed to do. Of course, this became a teachable moment for students to learn about access to elected leaders. The students, Sequoia and Frankie, did not expect a response knowing how busy the mayor's schedule must be. However, they were surprised when Mayor Salas agreed to an interview and met with them for more than 30 minutes.

Sequoia and Frankie shared their project at a showcase event one Saturday at their school. School board members, city council members, parents, and other community guests attended the showcase to learn from students about their issues and projects. Afterward, Sequoia and Frankie said they are definitely more inclined to get involved in leadership themselves and promote gender equality— especially knowing that they can reach out to state senators, congressional representatives, and other elected officials. I would say these students are on a positive trajectory for civic engagement.

If you have community partners to work with, think about how they might serve as "clients" for your students to learn from and develop products for in a project. Some local high schools do this to help students engage with community businesses, organizations, and nonprofits while helping those partners to address a need. For example, a local health clinic explained to students that many people in the community are suffering from treatable diseases and are not taking advantage of the free services provided by the clinic. Students worked in teams to conduct research in the community, develop ideas to address the problem, and then pitched their ideas in formal presentations to the health clinic staff. All of the students received valuable feedback about their research, ideas, and presentation skills. Some of the students got to see their ideas turned into campaigns in their community.

Think about the projects that your students are doing in your class. Are the projects reflective of their exploration and interaction with the larger community? Are there opportunities for community stakeholders to interact with your students as they present their projects and gather even more information? There are a variety of ways to infuse authenticity into student projects. Consider options in your planning, guidelines, and sharing.

Internships

Some schools have created robust job shadowing and internships for students to work with community leaders, businesses, and agencies. In most cases, internships organized by schools (mostly high schools) are unpaid and highly structured. These offer unique opportunities for students to see how the knowledge and skills learned in school are put to use in the world of work. Internships can be open-ended allowing for mentors to explain what they do and how their organization works. Students learn by shadowing, assisting, and doing work assigned to them. Or they can enter the internship with assignments from their teachers to look for certain things, explore particular tasks or queries, and keep logs or journals of their experiences.

When my son was in high school, he was provided a list of potential internships during his junior year. However, he wanted to obtain an internship with a particular nonprofit organization that aligned with his values as an environmentalist and whose work he admired. That organization was not on the list provided. With the school's approval, he contacted the organization's director and convinced him that an intern would benefit the organization. My son was so excited (and nervous) to start his internship. In the first week, he was given an assignment to research the names and contact information of local schools for their community outreach programs and create a spreadsheet listing the schools by district. Within a week, he handed his mentor the assignment. His mentor was baffled and said that the assignment was expected to take at least a month to complete. What my son learned was that his research and technology skills were much higher than anticipated by the director of this organization. He also learned how to advocate for what he wanted to achieve in the real world.

The results have been more than impressive!

Service learning is another avenue for aligning volunteer work in the community with academic goals found in the curriculum. Students have served their communities with clean-up events, visitations to veterans or senior living homes, house painting, habitat restoration, etc.

There are multiple ways to bring together your students and their larger communities. The two-way benefits build stronger relationships between schools and their communities as confidence grows for public education and our youth who will become the future leaders of that community. If authenticity starts in the heart, I say we go to the heart of our communities to unpack the learning context and recognize the value of social studies education.

CONCLUSION

Are you still climbing that ladder? I hope so. Too many excellent educators are leaving the field during this period known as the Great Resignation, which has also been called the "Big Quit" and "Great Reshuffle." Clearly, there is a lot about traditional education in the United States that needs reshuffled. However, we need the experience and institutional memory of veteran educators as well as the new and different perspectives of a new generation of teachers, some young in age and some bringing expertise from other fields into the world of education. We need to work together to apply important lessons from the global pandemic, January 6 Capitol insurrection, violence against Asian American and Pacific Islander citizens, and movements related to Black Lives Matter, #MeToo, LGBTQIA+ rights, mental health support, environmental justice, economic inequalities, and reproductive rights. This is the stuff of authentic social studies.

We live in a world of constant change and increasing ambiguity. Our abilities to navigate these changes and uncertainties rely on the knowledge, skills, and dispositions developed in an education system that attends to the humanities and elevates the role of social studies. Isn't this what we want for our students? They bring diversity of perspective and innovative ideas into a learning environment that requires critical and creative reasoning. Progress can and will be made when we nurture the curiosity and agency of students while they continue to learn history, geography, economics, civics and government in addition to other social sciences.

I realize that you might have many ideas swimming around in your brilliant and growing mind. If you are like me, you might appreciate a list of practical steps to get you moving in this lifelong journey of authentic education. The following is what I would write into the front page of my lesson plan book, but I encourage you to make your own list that supports you in the place where you find yourself as a teacher and sets manageable goals to get to the "next level."

To be an authentic teacher of social studies:

- Know yourself and remember why you entered teaching.
- Know your students, where they come from, and how they are.
- Be yourself and use your best judgment always in the classroom.
- Know that you will make mistakes. Embrace them as learning opportunities.
- Create a safe and brave space for students to explore, contribute, learn, and grow each day.
- Get to the heart of what you are teaching and help students understand why this is so important in today's world.
- Center humanity in your lessons and remember that social studies is all about people: who and how they are, the decisions they make, where they go and what they do, as well as their hopes and dreams.
- Help students see and develop their roles as global citizens, people who strive to make this world a better place (locally, nationally, globally).
- Reflect regularly on your own role, as a global citizen, with colleagues, and with students.

You might also think about how students are positioned in your classroom and work with them to develop intentions for making the most of your social studies class, which transfers to their roles and responsibilities as citizens of their communities, nation, and world.

For students to be authentic learners of social studies:

- Learn more about who you are and how you are connected to the world.
- Suspend assumptions and judgments about social studies and education.
- Actively listen to others as they share their experiences, ideas, and questions.
- Contribute your questions, ideas, and thoughts in every lesson.
- Be present and stay present
- Keep a curious mind.
- Look for connections to you, your family, your culture, and your communities.
- Find ways to apply what you are learning to your personal life.

As we learn more about our fellow human beings, we come to realize that people live with a multitude of differences (e.g., experiences, values, rights, privileges, nutrition, education levels, access to health care, etc.) and great similarities, too. The studies of humanity are complex and messy. We want to engage students and activate their social and emotional assets while helping them to understand without evaluation and judgment of others. Cooperation, conflict resolution, compromise, and community building are difficult to achieve when people are divided by prejudice, discrimination, racism, bigotry, and violence.

I was raised by a mother from China and a father of German descent. I learned to live in the "middle space" where I was not one or the other, but both. People tried to tell me what I was based on how they perceived me and I always took offense to that. Similarly, I grew up wanting to be a writer or a teacher. Fortunately, I have been able to carve out a life that allows me to be both. Here, I work in that "middle space." The middle space is an authentic space for me to live, learn, and thrive. Many students do not want to be told who they are or what they are. Most find themselves someplace between the labels ascribed by society. Let's help them to be their most authentic selves in our social studies classrooms and because of our social studies programs. You, too. Might you find yourself a more authentic person and educator by finding your own middle space?

I wish you the best in your ongoing journeys.

ACKNOWLEDGMENTS

I have always enjoyed many deep conversations about social studies and education with my incredible colleagues over the years, including Dr. Kevin Colleary, Dr. Walter Parker, Dr. James Banks, Katie Rosetti, Dr. Barbara Schubert, Dr. Roni Jones, Dr. Tom Herman, Amy Vigil, Matt Hayes, Barbara Vallejo Doten, Dr. Michelle Herczog, Mary Hendra, Nancy McTygue, Dr. Tuyen Tran, Toya Profit, Dawniell Black, and soon-to-be-doctor. Kelly Leon.

When Jared Taylor at Gibbs Smith Education contacted me about writing this book, our conversations rose to a level that challenged my thinking about where we have been in this field, where we find ourselves today, and where we need to go for the best possible future. Thank you, Jared, for resurfacing memories and fueling my passion for social studies education.

Finally, I remain incredibly grateful for my loving and supportive family. My son Evan continues to teach me about our fragile world, creative perspectives and pursuits, and the power of storytelling. My sister Christina takes care of me in ways that I don't recognize while immersed in writing, reading, and investigating. My mother Claire continues to nudge me in the direction of equity and high-quality education for every student who holds the potential for peace and justice in our world.

REFERENCES

Banks, J. (2019). *An introduction to multicultural education* (6th ed.). Pearson.

California Department of Education. (2016a). *Educating for global competency: Findings and recommendations from the 2016 California global education summit.*

California Department of Education. (2016b). *History-social science framework for California public schools.*

California Global Education Project. (2016). *Framework for global competence.*

Chopra, D. (2022). Deepak Chopra. https://www.deepakchopra.com

CNN. (2022). CNN 10. https://www.cnn.com/cnn10

College Board. (2022). Advanced Placement. https://ap.collegeboard.org/

Common Sense Media. (2022). Common Sense Media. https://www.commonsensemedia.org/

Gardner, H. (2006a). *Five minds for the future.* Harvard Business Review Press.

Gardner, H. (2006b). Multiple intelligences: New horizons. Basic Books.

Gardner, H. (2011). *Frames of mind: The theory of multiple intelligences* (3rd ed.). Basic Books.

Gay, G. (2000). *Culturally responsive teaching.* Teachers College Press.

Global Oneness Project. (2022). Global Oneness Project. https://www.globalonenessproject.org/

Harari, Y. N. (2018). 21 *Lessons for the 21st century.* Random House.

Hasso Plattner Institute of Design at Stanford University. (2022). Getting started with design thinking. https://dschool.stanford.edu resources/getting-started-with-design-thinking

International Baccalaureate. (2022). International Baccalaureate. https://www.ibo.org/

Kagan, S. (2022). Cooperative learning structures. https://www. kaganonline.com/free_articles/dr_spencer_kagan/426 Cooperative-Learning-Structures

KQED. (2022). Media literacy. https://www.kqed.org/education/media-literacy

Ladson-Billings, G. (2021). *Culturally relevant pedagogy: Asking a different question*. Teachers College Press.

Larmer, J., Ross, D., & Mergendollar, J. (2009). Project-based learning (PBL) starter kit. Buck Institute for Education.

Martin, D. (2012). *Reading like a historian: Teaching literacy in middle and high school history classrooms Aligned with common core state standards*. Teachers College Press.

McTygue, J., & Wiggins, G. (2005). *Understanding by design*. ASCD.

National Council for the Social Studies. (2002). *National standards for social studies teachers*.

National Council for the Social Studies. (2013). *The college, career, and civic life (C3) framework for social studies standards*.

National History Day. (2022). National History Day. https://www.nhd. org/

Newsela. (2022). Newsela. https://newsela.com

Newseum. (2022). Newseum. https://www.newseum.org/

NPR. (2022). Up First podcast. https://www.npr.org/podcasts/510318/ up-first

Paris, D. & Alim, H.S., (Eds.) (2017). *Culturally sustaining pedagogies: Teaching and learning for justice in a changing world*. Teachers College Press.

Prensky, M. (2010). *Teaching digital natives: Partnering for real learning*. Corwin.

Robinson, K. (2010). Changing education paradigms (TedTalk). https:// www.ted.com/talks/sir_ken_robinson_changing_education paradigms

Robinson, K. & Aronica, L. (2016). *Creative schools: The grassroots revolution that's transforming education*. Penguin Books.

Schell, E. (2003). *Exploring teachers experiences with the Colonial Williamsburg Teacher Institute*. University of San Diego.

Schell, E. & Fisher, D. (2006). *Teaching social studies: A literacy-based approach*. Pearson.

Stanford History Education Group. (2022). Civic online reasoning. https://cor.stanford.edu/

Tomlinson, C.A. (2014). *The differentiated classroom: Responding to the needs of all learners*. ASCD.

Tomlinson, C.A. & Sousa, D. (2018). *Differentiation and the brain: How neuroscience supports the learner-friendly classroom*. Solution Tree Press.

UC Regents. (2015). YPAR hub. http://yparhub.berkeley.edu/

Walqui, A. & Bunch, G. (2019). *Amplifying the curriculum: Designing quality learning opportunities for English learners*. Teachers College Press.

Wagner, T. (2008). *The global achievement gap: Why even our best schools don't teach the new survival skills our children need—and what we can do about it*. Basic Books.

World Savvy. (2022). World Savvy. https://www.worldsavvy.org/

Yosso, T.J. (2005). Whose culture has capital? *Race, Ethnicity and Education*, 8(1), 69–91. https://doi.org/10.1080/1361332052000341006

Zhao, Y. (2012). *World class learners: Educating creative and entrepreneurial students*. Corwin.

Zweirs, J. (2014). *Common core standards in diverse classrooms: Essential practices for developing academic language and disciplinary literacy*. Stenhouse.